MW00744566

How to Get Your Screen-Loving Kids to Read Books for Pleasure

How to Get Your Screen-Loving Kids to Read Books for Pleasure

KAYE NEWTON

© 2018 Kaye Newton

All rights reserved. No part of this book may be reproduced or transmitted in any form or by any means, electronic or mechanical, including photocopying or recording or by any information-storage-and-retrieval system, without written permission from the author. The names and identifying details of certain individuals have been changed to protect their privacy.

ISBN-13: 9780692986370
ISBN-10: 0692986375
Library of Congress Control Number: 2017917943
Linland Press, N. Charleston, SC

To Rick, and to everyone who promotes reading

Contents

Introduction

When I started the project described in this book, two of my children, ages eleven and fourteen, rarely read books for pleasure. They knew how to read and had been avid readers in elementary school. But by sixth grade, the year they entered middle school, books—just like Silly Bandz and ZhuZhu Pets—no longer interested them. (My youngest, age ten, enjoyed reading. But she did not yet own a smartphone, which can be a one-way ticket to reading dormancy.) My older children and their friends preferred to spend their free time playing Xbox Live, texting, and skimming social-media sites.

Since books have made every stage of my existence more enjoyable, while social media and Xbox Live have not, this bothered me. Selfishly, I wanted my adolescents to give books a chance to enhance their lives. While reading contributes to school success, I was also interested in promoting books because of the enjoyment and enrichment they offer.

But I wondered, could a regular parent like me, who is not a teacher, librarian, reading specialist, or tiger mom, lead her screen-loving children back to reading for pleasure? And could adolescents who claim, "I'm just not a reader," as they settle in front of their favorite Netflix series or *Overwatch* video game be transformed into readers? Was it possible for this metamorphosis to be painless, and perhaps even enjoyable?

The reading gurus say yes! Donalyn Miller, author of the best seller *The Book Whisperer*, points out that there is a reader in every adolescent, which the right conditions will let loose.[1] In an attempt to unleash my children's inner readers, I reused the tactics that originally got them interested in books. After all, none of us were born readers. We were shaped into them by parents, grandparents, caregivers, and teachers. Parents read *Goodnight Moon* to us before bed, and pre-school teachers enthusiastically chanted, "Brown bear, brown bear, what do you see?" School librarians matched books to our interests.

In order to determine which books could hook my teen and pre-teens on reading, I consulted family members, friends, librarians, and scores of Amazon reviews. I also asked my children, my nieces and nephews, and carpools of captive adolescents about books: What are you reading right now? What is the last good book you read? What do you want to read next? What would get you to read more?

Besides discussing books, I also observed how kids select what they want to read. During my family reading project, I concurrently ran a PTO fundraiser where I helped four hundred students choose books to donate to the school library. The books were spread out on multiple tables, and I could see which books the students fought over and which ones they wouldn't touch.

Finally, I road tested suggestions from the reading specialists cited at the back of this book. Much of their advice for encouraging reading was excellent, but some of it was impractical. While I like creative suggestions such as making a "Reading Boat" where your entire family curls up on a bed, pretends it's a catamaran, and reads together, that wouldn't work for us. My husband and son are both six feet five inches tall, and my daughters and I do not shop in the petite section (we are all over five foot eight). Our family Reading Boat would be overcrowded! The boat could collapse, or more likely, crew members would mutiny and push each other overboard.

The following pages detail practical ways to engage adolescents in reading for pleasure. I learned through trial and error that a tip that worked for one of my children wouldn't necessarily engage the others. I also found that reading tactics need to vary by season. Encouraging reading for pleasure during summer break was different from enhancing the enjoyment of required school reading.

After sixteen months of trying different strategies, I can report that all three of my children are reading more during their free time. Now, I don't mean that they are consuming *Great Expectations* or other literary works for fun. (They are currently reading Ally Condie's *Matched*; Nicola Yoon's *Everything, Everything*; and the graphic novel *Bad Island*, by Doug TenNapel.) Exploring Pip's expectations can be an exercise for their hardworking language-arts teachers. My kids continue to play video games, text, and download crazy-cat videos. Balancing screen time with books is an ongoing discussion in my house, but reading for pleasure is finally getting a fair share of my adolescents' attention.

Part 1
Understanding Reading
Motivations and Challenges

One

Why You Should Encourage Your Kids to Read for Pleasure

After I saw that the number of adolescent readers was dramatically declining, I hoped it was a mistake. But when I thought about the teen and preteens living in my own household, I recognized that the time they spent reading for pleasure dropped off at age eleven, when they entered middle school.

In my children's elementary school, there is a focused effort to make reading Fun, with a capital *F*. Teachers read aloud engaging stories during language-arts class. Parents bring in their favorite books to share with the students. There are book swaps at the holiday parties and free donuts at the book fairs. Students celebrate Dr. Seuss's birthday with streamers, read-alouds, and a pajama party. Kids look forward to their weekly Library Day, where they self-select engaging books and graphic novels.

In middle school, the reading experience changes. In order to meet state testing standards, students read informational texts and textbooks. The entire class reads a chapter a night of a book such as Steinbeck's *The Grapes of Wrath* or Orwell's *Animal Farm*. Students are required to annotate each page of a chapter. Annotating, as my son points out, "ruins the flow of a story." Besides annotating, middle-school students analyze the required reading. They analyze the main characters, they analyze imagery, and they analyze each other's analysis. One student told me, "I liked reading until I was forced to overthink every sentence."

Typically, more homework is assigned in middle school than in elementary school. Between studying, sports, school clubs, and vigilantly maintaining an Instagram account, the students have less time for reading. And to top it all off, by the spring of sixth grade, students may acquire smartphones and "boyfriends" or "girlfriends." These relationships are conducted almost entirely through their phone screens, requiring no eye or physical contact (a relief to parents), but do involve sending hundreds of time-consuming texts and heart emojis.

In high school, teens are even busier. They juggle studying, sports, jobs, driving, school clubs, SAT prep, dating, college applications, and expanding social-media accounts. And reading takes another hit. One mom told me that her sixteen-year-old daughter is so busy with activities and schoolwork that "she doesn't have time to make her bed," let alone enjoy a novel.

This trend is reflected in the following sad statistics from Common Sense Media's "Children, Teens, and Reading" 2014 research brief:

- 53 percent of nine-year-olds versus 17 percent of seventeen-year-olds are daily readers.
- The proportion of children who "never" or "hardly ever" read tripled from 1984 to 2014. A third of thirteen-year-olds and 45 percent of seventeen-year-olds say they've read for pleasure one to two times a year, if that.

While time-consuming extracurriculars and loads of homework contribute to this slide in reading, many parents and teachers suspect that the siren call of video games and social media is the main culprit. The pinging of Snapchats and texts whizzing back and forth through cyberspace is exciting. The gratification of receiving 230 "likes" on a duck-face pose is addictive. After flipping through tweets and chats until their pupils turn into spinning rectangles, adolescents can find it difficult to concentrate on a complicated paragraph or long sentence cemented on the page.

Reading a book for pleasure can be an unwelcome challenge to a preteen who contentedly plays *Super Mario* on his phone for hours every day. As parents, we recognize that reading is a good thing, but we may look at our screen-loving adolescent as he makes Mario jump up for coins and think, "Why disrupt his current peaceful state by suggesting he put down his cell phone and pick up a book? This is his downtime, and he seems so relaxed. Mario makes him happy." You may know from personal experience that your son does not like to be disturbed midgame. Why set yourself up for an extended eye roll or a snippy remark? And who knows—after playing *Super Mario* for six hours a day, 365 days a year, isn't it possible, maybe even likely, that your preteen could be acquiring some kind of dormant computer skill that will blossom later in life, transforming him into a famous and talented video-game designer?

While we all hope for the best, the reality is that everyone, including budding app creators, needs to balance screen time with reading the long-form text found in books and articles. It's telling that many of the Silicon Valley executives who create smartphones and apps strictly limit their own kids' screen time and encourage reading. (See the *New York Times* article "Steve Jobs Was a Low-Tech Parent," September 10, 2014.) Like people from all walks of life, they recognize that we acquire the skills necessary to do well in school, the workplace, and life through thinking about what we read. While the Internet and apps can be crucial in accessing and organizing information, employers want people who can solve problems, critically reason, and communicate in writing. Reading well is necessary to attain all these skills.

Books and their compatriots deserve a fair share of our adolescents' attention. One could argue, as author James Patterson does in his article "How to Raise a Fanatical Reader," that encouraging reading is a parental responsibility. It's like teaching your teens to parallel park or to cease slurping milk directly out of their cereal bowls. While they may not appreciate your interactions now, down the line, they will.

Smartphones and other screens are very capable of seizing a large share of teens' and preteens' time. We need to stand up for books, graphic novels, magazines, and other content that involves comprehending sequential sentences. It's not hard to do, and it can be enjoyable. The following section explains why we should make the effort.

How Reading Helps Teens and Preteens

The benefits of reading have been widely studied. Here are some of them:

1. ***Reading reduces stress.*** Who, in this day and age of constant newsfeeds featuring natural disasters and rabble-rousing politicians, does not need to de-stress? According to a 2009 University of Sussex study, reading for just six minutes a day has been shown to reduce stress levels by 68 percent. Reading silently for six minutes slowed down participants' heart rates and eased muscle tension. (It doesn't matter what type of book you read, it just needs to be one that you enjoy.) Author Frank

Bruni reports that he and his friends find reading before bed is similar to meditating: "If we spend our last hours or minutes of the night reading rather than watching television, we wake the next morning with thoughts less jumbled, moods less jangled. Reading has bequeathed what meditation promises."[1] And for most of us, it's easier to read a book than pretzel our mind into a Zen state.

2. *Reading makes people smarter. It improves our concentration, memory, analytical skills, writing, and general knowledge.* When we learn information from a book or an article, our brains get a workout. Different areas of the brain—like the parts for vision, memory, and language—function together to read sentences, comprehend words, and construct mental images. This process builds concentration and memory.[2]

Maryanne Wolf, director of the Center for Reading and Language Research at Tufts University and author of *Proust and the Squid: The Story and Science of the Reading Brain,* points out, "Typically when you read, you have more time to think. Reading gives you a unique pause button for comprehension and insight. By and large, with oral language—when you watch a film or listen to a tape—you don't press pause."

We gain knowledge from books. University of California, Berkeley, professor Anne Cunningham points out in her article "What Reading Does for the Mind" that reading contributes to increased vocabulary, general knowledge, and verbal fluency. In addition, reading helps people spot patterns faster, which is associated with better analytical thinking.[3] Donalyn Miller agrees; she writes, "We teachers have more than enough anecdotal evidence that the students who read the most are the best spellers, writers, and thinkers. No exercise gives more instructional bang for the buck than reading."[4]

3. ***Reading develops empathy.*** When we read books or listen to audiobooks with well-developed characters, we slip into the minds of those characters. We learn to understand what someone else is thinking and feeling. For example, as adolescents read Sharon Draper's *Out of My Mind*, they experience firsthand the main character's frustration that she is unable to walk or speak.

The *Journal of Applied Social Psychology* reports that novels like those in the *Harry Potter* series can help people understand what others feel and reduce prejudices. In a press release, Dr. Loris Vezzali, the lead author of the study, explains, "Harry Potter empathizes with characters from stigmatized categories, tries to understand their sufferings, and to act towards social equality." As readers, we experience Harry's compassion and become more compassionate.

4. ***Reading helps teens sleep better.*** Pediatricians recommend that teenagers get nine to ten hours of sleep a night. Is this happening in your house? Mine neither. My children leave for school at 6:30 a.m. Their alarms ring at 5:45 a.m. Ten hours of sleep would require them to go to bed at 7:45 p.m., which they have not done since the third grade.

Since sleep is essential to healthy brain development, adolescents need whatever sleep they get to be high quality. According to Michael Breus, a fellow of the American Academy of Sleep Medicine, "The brain's prefrontal cortex—responsible for complex thinking and decision-making, as well as emotional regulation—is among the last areas of the brain to develop, and undergoes significant maturation during the teenage years. This part of the brain is especially sensitive to the effects of sleep deprivation."[5] Lack of high-quality sleep can lead to poor performance in school and on the sports field, as well as serious safety issues like drowsy driving.[6]

Using technology before bed can negatively affect a person's quality of sleep and how long he or she sleeps. Light from screens reduces the production of melatonin, which is the hormone that helps control the sleep cycle.

By creating a bedtime ritual of reading a book before bed instead of checking a smartphone, adolescents can improve their sleep quality and fall asleep faster.

5. ***Reading prepares teens for college and the workplace.*** Reading expert Penny Kittle, author of *Book Love*, reports that college students need to read between two hundred and six hundred pages per week to be successful. Reading comprehension and speed, like many skills, improve with practice. The more teens read in high school, the better prepared they are for college work.

Many high-school students read two-page SparkNotes summaries instead of a three-hundred-page assigned novel. (SparkNotes and its competitor Shmoop offer free plot overviews of books as well as analyses of themes and characters.) And SparkNotes is popular. According to a 2011 poll done by Cherry Hill High School, 87 percent of its students use SparkNotes. However, SparkNotes and Shmoop aren't going to get teens through college courses. Professors want in-depth analysis and interpretations of the articles and papers they assign, most of which aren't reviewed by SparkNotes.

And it's not just professors who require strong reading skills. Employers need employees who can read and write well. According to the Conference Board surveys, employers rank reading comprehension as an essential skill for workplace success.[7] Business news, surveys, marketing materials, customer reviews, and endless work-related e-mails need to be comprehended by employees. The National Endowment for the Arts reports, "Reading for pleasure is strongly correlated to academic achievement, increased employment opportunities, and civic engagement."[8]

6. ***Reading can connect generations.*** Grandparents are eager to bond with adolescent grandkids. But the two groups may have dissimilar interests. Grandpa likes to discuss his golf handicap, politics, and the Weather Channel, none of which pique the interest of his preteen granddaughters. They want to chat about Selena Gomez's new Instagram account, and why she keeps regressing to date Justin Bieber. Fortunately, books, a familiar medium to both generations, can be a catalyst for conversations.

    This may come as a surprise: 55 percent of the people who read young adult (YA) books are over the age of eighteen.[9] Many grandparents enjoy consuming novels like R. J. Palacio's *Wonder*, the *Harry Potter* series, *The Hunger Games*, *The Chronicles of Narnia*, and anything their grandchild recommends.

7. ***Reading may help people live longer.*** Reading a book for as little as half an hour a day increases your personal "survival advantage" (PSA) over nonreaders. Researchers at Yale University report in the journal *Social Science and Medicine* (September 2016) that "the benefits of reading books include a longer life in which to read them." When compared with adults who read no books, the group that read up to 3.5 hours a week was 17 percent less likely to die over the follow-up period. Results were even better for those who read for over 3.5 hours every week; their PSA was 27 percent higher than that of the nonreaders.

Two

UNDERSTANDING THE TYPES OF READERS AND PROMOTING READING

Besides understanding the benefits of reading, it's helpful to learn about the types of teen and preteen readers and what motivates them to pick up a book. Many parents ask, "Is my child just not a reader? Are some children born readers, and others born PlayStation gamers?"

Year after year, teachers, librarians, and parents witness children who say they hate reading become engaged readers when they find the right book. Every person has the potential to enjoy reading. Seniors in high school and college, and even those who've already graduated from college, can discover a love of books. During a parent-teacher conference, a talented Teacher of the Year recipient mentioned to me that she didn't enjoy reading until after college, when she fell in love with bonnet-ripping Amish romance novels.

If your adolescent enjoys movies and television shows, then he or she appreciates a story. Storytelling has been around since humans first walked the earth, and it's hardwired into all of us. To enjoy reading, we just need to find the stories—fiction and nonfiction—that appeal to us.

While every adolescent has the potential to become an engaged reader, they can all start at different places. Parents of twins and multiple children recognize that some kids fall into reading more easily than others. One child may be a devoted reader, and his sibling may struggle to finish a comic book. A father of identical twin twelve-year-old boys pointed out to me that his son Jack is a devoted reader whose twin brother, Sam, has to be tethered to a couch next to a watchful parent before he will open a book.

Jack reads in his desk during math class and talks excitedly about John Green's latest novel in the same way his peers discuss Jay-Z's recent album drop. Sam is a dormant reader; he can read but chooses not to during his free time. Sam completes school assignments but does not read on the weekends, holidays, or summer break. When asked why he doesn't read for pleasure, Sam explains that "books are boring" and asks, "Why read when you can watch?" He also points out that he is too busy with activities, sports, and school to read a book for fun. Every dormant reader can become an engaged reader. They just need to find the right high-interest books and the time to read them.

What Promoting Reading Looks Like

Between work, hauling kids to extracurricular activities, grocery shopping, and managing a household, many of us have our hands full. We wonder, "Do I really have to get involved with this? Can't my kids' teachers encourage them to read? Isn't it their job?"

Teachers need our help! Public-school teachers are pressured to teach to the standardized tests their students are required to take. Educational initiatives mandate that students spend more time reading "informational texts" such as presidential speeches, scientific papers, and train schedules. There is less classroom time available for free reading and encouraging reading for pleasure. In addition, teachers are busy instructing students on the mechanics of reading. They teach fluency, which is the ability to read with accuracy and speed; and reading comprehension, which is the skill of understanding what you read.

While teachers focus on instruction, it's up to parents (and grandparents, babysitters, aunts, and uncles) to help adolescents encounter great books and to actually read them. Jim Trelease points out in *The Read Aloud Handbook* that "children spend 900 hours a year in school and 7,800 hours outside of school. Which teacher has the bigger influence? Where is there more time available for change?"

Encouraging reading is our job. When you connect with your kids over a book, you learn about their views and opinions. It's a small-time commitment for a big payoff.

Here is what a week of encouraging reading can look like:

- While picking up a book at our public library that I reserved for myself, I grab the third book in Rick Yancy's 5th Wave trilogy, which my youngest requested. (She is in a yearlong dystopian phase, where there is never a shortage of oppressive governments or incompetent adults.) I also check out graphic novels my son might like and pick up an extra copy of *A Long Way Gone*, which my son is reading for school. Estimated time: fourteen minutes.
- I read the back cover and first five pages of *A Long Way Gone*, a true story about a boy soldier in Sierra Leone, while waiting in the school parking lot to pick up the kids. I chat with my son about the book while driving. Estimated time: seven minutes.

- I shut down the Xbox and let my son know that he has the opportunity to earn a half hour of video gaming if he reads for a half hour too. I ignore his grumbling. Estimated time: two minutes a day for five days, or ten minutes total.
- I print out newspaper articles about scientists who are attempting to contact aliens, a former classmate who made $10,000 selling cupcakes, and a review of the upcoming movie *Blade Runner 2049*. I read parts of the articles at dinner. Estimated time: thirteen minutes.
- I ask my kids which book they are carrying in their backpack for their school's sustained silent reading, where they read a book of their choice for thirty minutes. Estimated time: two minutes.

In sum, I spent 46 out of the 10,800 minutes of my week promoting reading. Apart from policing video games, which I wish were never invented, I enjoyed all those minutes. I discovered a new good book (*A Long Way Gone*) and that I will go see *Blade Runner 2049*.

But enough about me; let's answer a few commonly asked questions that you may have about your role in promoting reading.

What if my partner and I are not readers? We prefer to spend our downtime watching HBO shows and Netflix. Do we have to model reading to get our preteen daughter to open a book?

Our kids watch us closely; they do what we do. The more interest and enthusiasm we show in reading, the better. Preteens and teens are particularly sensitive to anything that smacks of "unfairness." (It's not effective to direct your preteen to read a hundred pages of a novel while you binge-watch *Breaking Bad* from the living room couch.) Among the most powerful predictors of whether children will be frequent readers is whether their parents are frequent readers.

Start by reading something in front of your child. It could be any-thing that interests you, such as a *People* magazine exposé, an article about your dream vacation, or the Brookstone catalog. Read two or three paragraphs out loud to your kid and talk about what you read. (Try to do this at least every other day.) You can read anywhere—over dinner or breakfast, or in the car before you turn on the engine. Leave articles, magazines, or catalogs on the table or in the car for your daughter to finish reading on her own.

Here are some additional ideas:

Read a chapter or, better yet, an entire YA (young adult) book that your kid is reading. (See chapter 6 for books that hook teens and preteens. Many of these are great reads for both adolescents and adults.) Converse with your daughter about the book. Ask questions. What does she like about the story? Who is her favorite character? What does she think of the ending?

Find a reading buddy for your kid. A reading buddy is anyone who enjoys talking about books. It can be a grandparent, cousin, sibling, school friend, or babysitter. Take your adolescent and read-ing buddy to the library or bookstore, where they are surrounded by books. Encourage your adolescent to check out or buy a book. Include a coffee drink, frozen yogurt, or smoothie at the end of the outing. (See the upcoming section on people—besides you—who can encourage your kid to read.)

Television shows based on books can get kids reading. Google a list of TV series based on young adult books. Watch the first epi-sode, and then encourage your kid to read the books to find out what happens. You could do this with Lemony Snicket's *A Series of Unfortunate Events*. Parents report that their fourteen-year-old daughters who were obsessed with the TV show *Pretty Little Liars* would agree to read some of the books if it meant they got to watch the next episode.

My twelve-year-old, who once loved reading, recently said she hated books. During a parent-teacher conference, I expressed my concern over this. The teacher replied that I should just relax; the joy of reading would eventually return to my daughter. Should I sit back and wait for this to happen?

When I sat back for a year and did nothing to promote reading books, my kids doubled down on their screen time. While they became more proficient at *Madden NFL* and Words with Friends, virtually no reading for pleasure occurred. The draw of technology is irresistible for most adolescents. If you want your daughter to experience the joys and benefits of reading, be proactive. Utilize the upcoming tips and suggestions.

I've read that boys' reading-comprehension skills are dropping faster than girls'. Any advice about encouraging boys to read?

Research indicates that girls tend to read more books than boys and possess stronger reading skills, and this gender gap may be increasing.[1] Teachers and librarians are aware of this and are looking for ways to better engage boys in reading.

Every boy and girl is one captivating book away from becoming a reader. So what are the books that enthrall boys? Many boys enjoy action-packed books with a male main character. On his Guys Read website, author Jon Scieszka suggests that we "let boys know that nonfiction reading is reading. Magazines, newspapers, websites, biographies, science books, comic books, graphic novels are all reading material."

Start by building on what your son likes, and let him choose what he wants to read. Here are some ideas:

For video gamers: *Diary of a Minecraft Zombie, Ender's Game,* and *Ready Player One* are good choices. Nonfiction books like *Game On!,* which describes the latest video games and how to win them, and the *Guinness World Records 2017 Gamer's Edition* can also appeal to the gamer in your life.

For preteen boys who like to laugh: Try the *Diary of a Wimpy Kid* series, the *Big Nate* series, Roald Dahl books, Calvin and Hobbes, and David Walliams's books like the *Demon Dentist*. Preteens also like joke books such as *Jokelopedia*. (Brace yourself for the impending onslaught of "why did the chicken cross the road" jokes.) Older teens may chuckle when reading *The Hitchhiker's Guide to the Galaxy*, Terry Pratchett's Discworld books, and *Good Omens*. David Sedaris's books and Dave Barry's columns are hilarious.

For fans of Marvel comics and Star Wars: Does your son enjoy the movies based on Marvel comics, like X-Men? If so, try graphic novels with lots of action such as *Batman: The Killing Joke* or a paperback like *X-Men Days of Future Past.* Eighth graders and older teens may enjoy Brandon Sanderson's unconventional superhero Steelheart trilogy. For Star Wars fans, check out visual dictionaries of the characters and planets as well as Timothy Zahn's books like *Star Wars: Thrawn* and Michael Stackpoles's Star Wars: X-Wing series.

For sports fans: Mike Lupica's Home Team series and Tim Green's Football Genius series depict issues boys face on and off the field. Kwame Alexander's *Crossover* and *Booked*, which are written in verse, are popular with basketball fans. Older teens may enjoy *The Blind Side* or *Moneyball*, by Michael Lewis. Also, try *Sports Illustrated* and *ESPN Magazine* and biographies of their favorite players.

For those that enjoy fantasy and adventure: Try *Harry Potter*; anything by Rick Riordan; the Leviathan trilogy, by Scott Westerfeld; the *Ranger's Apprentice* series; and Tolkien's *The Lord of the Rings*. Brandon Sanderson's high-fantasy Mistborn series may appeal to ages fourteen and up. If your son enjoys creepy dystopian tales, try Neal Shusterman's Unwind trilogy.

For action and thriller fans: Try the *Alex Rider* series, by Anthony Horowitz; the Maze Runner series; the Michael Vey series, by Richard Paul Evans; and *Cherub: The Recruit*, by British writer Robert Muchamore. Older, mature teens may enjoy Lee Child's *Jack Reacher* series or David Baldacci's books. Many of these books have been made into movies. If possible, have them read the book before watching the movie.

For adolescents who love speed: Check out the Harley-Davidson catalog, *Jeff Gordon: His Dream, Drive & Destiny* by Joe Garner (fourteen and up), and *Muscle Car Review* (single-issue magazine).

For boys interested in history: Check out Steve Sheinkin's books like *Bomb: The Race to Build—and Steal—the World's Most Dangerous Weapon*; the young adult version of *Unbroken*; or *Chasing Lincoln's Killer*, by James Swanson. Younger teens enjoy the *I Survived* series, by Lauren Tarshis; the *Horrible History* series, by Terry Deary; and the *Who Was?* biography series.

In addition to enjoying books that reflect their interests, boys respond positively to male reading models. The British Parliament's Boys' Reading Commission stated in its 2012 report that in order to narrow the reading gender gap, every boy should have weekly support from a male reading model.

Author Jim Trelease agrees and points out that many dads focus on developing their sons' athletic abilities rather than their reading skills. Fathers and sons spend hours together at the gym or batting cages, but how about Dad also takes his son to the library or bookstore? How about they sit on the couch and read their respective books and magazines? While we all like to dream, it's highly unlikely that our kids will play professional sports or receive a Nike contract. But they will need to read and write well to succeed in the workplace.

It's not just dads who can mentor boys. Grandpa can read a few pages of the book his grandson is currently reading and talk to him about it. Or an older male cousin can read an article with your son. If Dad (or Grandpa or another reading mentor) lives far away or travels extensively, he can text, e-mail, and Skype about books and send links to articles.

Three

Reading with Learning Differences

Adolescents with learning differences like ADHD and dyslexia find it helpful to "ear read" with audiobooks. Audiobooks, which are books read by human narrators, and text-to-speech books, which are read by computers, count as real reading. Like print books and e-books, audiobooks teach vocabulary words and character development. Many have award-winning narrators who do a terrific job depicting the character voices and making them come to life.

Teens and preteens can listen to books on their phones or iPads. Reading the book while listening along to the narrator helps adolescents with comprehension and pronunciation. Logging on to Audible or YouTube and reading along with a narrator enables kids to stay focused on plot and characters. Services like Bookshare and Learning Ally provide the audio version of almost any book or article from teen chick-lit, like Jenny Han's *To All the Boys I've Loved Before*, to *Harvard Law Review* articles on the right to privacy.

Adolescents with learning differences need support at home and school. Parents, you are your kid's reading advocate. Don't wait around for the school to address learning differences. If you suspect your child has an issue, talk to his or her teacher and ask for an evaluation. Before your kid can get help from a reading specialist, public schools require a full evaluation. See Understood.org for more details on this process and how to write a letter to the school requesting a free evaluation.

Reading specialists teach a variety of comprehension and decoding techniques. Daily practice—like reading at home for twenty minutes—is a key component in implementing the strategies taught at school. It's up to parents and caregivers to make sure daily reading happens. Adolescents with learning differences often enjoy "hi-lo books"—high-interest books written at a lower reading level.

Websites such as Understood.org and Scholastic.com list hi-lo books for adolescents. There are publishers like Orca that produce hi-lo books for developing readers. These books have a low page count, large amounts of white space, slightly larger font, and plots that are easy to follow but that engage teens. They often have an edgy cover, so they resemble the YA books peers are reading. The low page count and basic vocabulary of hi-lo books enable an emerging reader to finish a novel with confidence.

There is a wide array of information for parents of kids with learning differences. Here are some helpful websites:

- Reading Rockets (http://www.readingrockets.org). Reading Rockets offers information about how parents can help struggling readers. They have a page called "Targeting the Problem" that describes specific reading issues like fluency or vocabulary and how to address them.
- Understood (https://www.understood.org). This nonprofit's goal is to help parents who have children with learning and attention issues. Understood has articles on supporting your

child's reading at home, partnering with your kid's school, and IEP plans, among many other topics.

- DyslexiaHelp (http://dyslexiahelp.umich.edu). This website is provided by the University of Michigan and contains tips and ideas, activities, success stories, and up-to-date information about dyslexia.
- The Yale Center for Dyslexia & Creativity (http://www.dyslexia.yale.edu). This site focuses on the strengths of those with dyslexia and offers research and practical information for parents and children.
- Learning Ally (https://www.learningally.org). Learning Ally is a large audiobook database, with over seventy-five thousand digitally recorded books in audio format. Kids with learning differences can read along while listening to books.
- Bookshare (https://www.bookshare.org). Bookshare is an online library that encourages reading and listening with e-books in audio, Braille, large font, and more.

My daughter is in eighth grade and reading at fifth-grade level. She feels like there is no point in trying to read since she will never catch up to her peers. How can I encourage her?

Reassure your daughter that everyone struggles with some types of text. Even teachers, professors, and other skilled readers have trouble comprehending certain books. (Just scan the Goodreads.com reviews of James Joyce's *Finnegans Wake* to see their confusion and frustration.) Also, point out that it's not as hard to move up reading grade levels as it sounds. It's not the same as skipping a grade in school. Teachers report that they have students who move up three or more reading levels within a school year. It could take your daughter twelve months or less of daily reading practice at home and instruction at school for her to be reading at her grade level.

While teachers and specialists will support your daughter, don't leave it all up to them. Communicate with her teacher. Inquire how you can help. Ask for an evaluation if it hasn't been done. If your daughter has a learning difference like dyslexia, check out the previous pages for resources. Then make sure you have plenty of engaging reading material at home that is on her reading level. Get high-interest–low-vocabulary (hi-lo) books and graphic novels from the library. Here are some suggestions: Raina Telgemeier's graphic novels like *Smile* and *Sisters*; *Diary of a Wimpy Kid* books; Lauren Tarshis's *I Survived* series; the *Who Was?* biography series with the giant bobble-head covers; the Amulet series, by Kazu Kibuishi; and the *Wake* trilogy, by Lisa McMann.

When my youngest learned to read, it helped to take a break if she got tired of the process. After switching to an activity that she enjoyed, like kicking the soccer ball or making banana bread, she returned to reading in a positive—or at least neutral—state of mind. Reducing the reading sessions into ten- or fifteen-minute segments and pointing out sentences that she read well also helped. Congratulating her when she completed a book or chapter made the process more pleasant. Also, rereading part of a favorite book, magazine, or catalog with her at the end of a session reinforces that reading is fun.

My adolescents told me that reading is for "nerds" and they would be embarrassed if their classmates saw them reading books. How do I respond to this?

How about referring your kids to the *Urban Dictionary* (*UD*) definitions of a "nerd"? The *UD* explains that a nerd is "one whose IQ exceeds his weight" and "the person you will one day call 'Boss.'" In this day and age, nerds (a.k.a. smart people who read) are living large. Have your kids seen pictures of Bill Gates's home, with its sixty-foot pool and underwater stereo system? How about the customized Tesla that Elon Musk drives and his company produces? Like many successful people who own the stuff that teens consider "cool," Gates and Musk are both big readers. (Gates reads fifty books a year.[1] Elon Musk will go through two books in one day, according to his brother.[2]) Are your adolescents *Hamilton* fans? (If not, download the soundtrack, and they will be.) *Hamilton*, the hit musical, was born when Lin-Manuel Miranda read a biography of Alexander Hamilton *for fun during his vacation.* Miranda's whole life changed because of one book.

Encourage your kids to read for all its mind-expanding benefits. If they are uncomfortable reading a paperback on the school bus because they may get teased, they can read discreetly on their cell phones or iPads or listen to an audiobook via earbuds. They can always read in the privacy of your home.

Could my preteen hate to read because she has vision issues?

Possibly. If an adolescent has a vision problem or light sensitivity, it can make reading a challenge. The Vision Council of America recommends that kids have their eyes checked annually by an optometrist or optometrist. Some of the signs of vision issues are squinting, closing one eye, seeing double letters, or headaches when reading. If your kid is exhibiting any of these signs or mentions that she can't see the whiteboards at school, get her eyes checked. Sometimes kids with reading challenges have visual-processing issues that can cause them to see a *p* as a *q* or cause difficulty in finding a number on a page. These can be diagnosed and addressed by a pediatric ophthalmologist or a pediatric optometrist.

Four

What Counts as "Real" Reading?

Today's screen-loving teens and preteens read more words than previous generations. But many of these words are abbreviated text speak. (Txts r not RR!) It's helpful to have an understanding of the different types of reading material available to adolescents and what constitutes "real" long-form reading. Here are common questions parents ask:

My teen reads texts, GroupMe, Snapchats, Instagram posts, tweets, and other social-media sites. Does that count as "real" reading?

No, that does not as "real" long-form reading. Snapchat, tweets, GroupMe, and texts count as scattered, skim reading, not long-form, sequential reading. Teens scour sites, videos, tweets, messages, and photos, flipping between them every six seconds. They get tiny, superficial views on a variety of topics, interrupted by dozens of chats or snaps buzzing into their phone.

"Reading a book, and taking the time to ruminate and make inferences and engage the imaginational processing, is more cognitively enriching, without doubt, than the short little bits that you might get if you're into the 30-second digital mode," said Ken Pugh, a cognitive neuroscientist at Yale who has studied brain scans of children reading.[1] Book reading or listening to an audiobook demands concentration and imagination that social media does not.

Teachers, professors, and employers report that while the iPhone generation is good at finding and distributing information quickly, they are challenged by in-depth reading and analysis. Professors notice that many of their college students skim long articles and focus on the surface meaning of what they skimmed. As a result, students miss the facts from the middle of the article as well as deeper meanings. Employers say that it's a challenge finding recent college grads with the adequate critical-thinking skills that reading develops. According to a recent PayScale poll of over sixty-three thousand managers, 60 percent of the managers surveyed felt that recent grads did not have the critical-thinking and problem-solving skills to do their jobs well.[2]

Screen skimming should be balanced with in-depth book and article reading. We all need to practice the focused concentration that reading and thinking about a book requires.

My kids only want to read the *Dork Diaries* series and Godzilla graphic novels for pleasure. Should I encourage them to read something more substantial, like Newbery Medal–winning novels?

Kids need to choose the books they read for pleasure. Doing so helps them learn how to decide which books they like, builds their confidence, and motivates them to finish a book.

Your child's fixation on Godzilla is a stage. What preteens read now is not where they will end up. Their tastes will change and develop. Teachers will encourage your kids to read more complex books over time. Our role as parents is to keep them on the reading ladder, and if Godzilla graphic novels can do that, great. Let them binge on Godzilla or the Dork Diaries. Then encourage your kids to check out their associated read-alikes.

Author Ann Patchett points out, "I'm all for reading bad books because I consider them to be a gateway drug. People who read bad books now may or may not read better books in the future. People who read nothing now will read nothing in the future."[3]

Keep in mind it doesn't matter if we loved *Wuthering Heights* as a preteen but our twelve-year-old daughters are addicted to Lisi Harrison's fashion-frenemy-focused the Clique series. This is not about us and our tastes. Your preteen doesn't care if you were swept away by Heathcliff and Cathy running wild through the misty English moors; she wants to read what appeals to her. The Clique's mall-dwelling, boy-chasing, backstabbing girl drama intrigues thousands of readers. Eventually, adolescents grow out of the Clique and into other books like John Green's well-written fiction about high-school relationships. The point is that your kids are reading, which is a good thing.

Author Neil Gaiman agrees that children should just be encouraged to open a book. In his 2013 Reading Agency lecture, Gaiman warns, "Well-meaning adults can destroy a child's love of reading: stop them reading what they enjoy, or give them worthy-but-dull books you like…you'll wind up with a generation convinced reading is uncool and, worse, unpleasant."

What about watching the movie or TV version of the book? Isn't it almost the same as reading the book?

No, it's not the same. Reading the written word or listening to a book on tape requires your brain to imagine what the characters, settings, and scenes look like. You create mental pictures; it's an active process. When you watch a film or TV series, the pictures of the people and places are laid out for you on the screen. You are receiving the results of the film director's and actors' interpretation of the screenplay of the book.

Reading the book before watching the screen version gives you the opportunity to visualize the characters and settings first. The book usually contains more details and information than the movie, and people tend to enjoy the book more. Whenever possible, insist that your kids read the book before seeing the screen version.

My teens read SparkNotes, which provides online book summaries, instead of reading an assigned book for class. They are tired, busy, and stressed and say they need the online help. Does "SparkNoting" count as reading?

SparkNoting in lieu of reading an assigned book counts as reading someone else's analysis and summary, instead of doing the work of reading, thinking, and arriving at your own conclusions. As mentioned earlier, your kids are not alone in their use of SparkNotes. Students use SparkNotes to write papers, complete homework assignments, and study for tests. As one adolescent pointed out, "It's better if I read the book; but I use SparkNotes because it's easy."

Most teachers are familiar with SparkNotes and Shmoop, which also offers book summaries. They try to design their tests and quizzes to avoid receiving regurgitated SparkNote answers from their students. Instructors point out that SparkNoting is like trying to get in shape by watching someone else lift weights; you aren't going to build muscle by watching your friend work out on a Bowflex machine. Students need to do the work of reading and analyzing to build these skills. Mention this to your teen, along with the fact that SparkNoting is associated with an increased risk of plagiarism.

While teachers generally discourage the use of SparkNotes, they occasionally make an exception when it comes to decoding Shakespeare's language. SparkNotes' No Fear Shakespeare guides make plays like *Hamlet* more accessible to students by translating the text into the regular English spoken today.[4] Once students understand the language, they can discuss the play's characters and themes.

Do graphic novels count as real reading?

Graphic novels, which look like comic books but are the length of novels, are considered by many teachers, librarians, and Scholastic.com as real reading. (Note: The word "graphic" in this case does not mean "adult," "rated R," or an E. L. James story. "Graphic" means "highly illustrated.") While parents (myself included) question whether books that are 90 percent drawings and 10 percent text count as real reading, experts remain steadfast in their support of graphic novels.

Librarians and teachers insist that not only can graphic novels drive students toward reading books, but they also stand on their own merits. (In my experience, graphic novels lead my son to read more graphic novels, so he needs to balance them with picture-free chapter books.)

There are graphic novels in multiple genres on almost any subject, from modern female superheroes to the classics like Gareth Hinds's *The Odyssey* to *Maus*, a graphic novel about the Holocaust that won the Pulitzer Prize. Graphic novels' visual appeal is part of their draw. Scholastic.com reports in its 2015 *A Guide to Using Graphic Novels with Children and Teens*, "School librarians and educators have reported outstanding success getting kids to read with graphic novels, citing particularly their popularity with reluctant readers, especially boys—a group traditionally difficult to reach." Schools and libraries recognize the growing popularity of graphic novels and are building up their collections.

What is "manga"? Does that count as reading?

Manga (rhymes with Topanga and the block-crashing game Jenga) are Japanese comics or graphic novels, which many reading experts and librarians consider real reading. Manga is usually in black and white, read backward or right to left, and often features aspects of Japanese culture. These books are extremely popular in Japan and can be written for adults, teens, or younger kids.

YALSA, the Young Adult Library Services branch of the American Library Association, recently posted an article on engaging young adults by reading picture books to them. My kid stopped reading picture books in the second grade. Are picture books now considered real reading for teens?

The YALSA October 13, 2017, article "Picture Books for Young Adults" explains how librarians can use picture books like *A Hungry Lion* or *Mr. Maxwell's Mouse* in their teen programs. It suggests that librarians engage teens by reading the picture books aloud or that they "incorporate picture books into book clubs. Try passing a picture book with YA appeal around the book group, having each person read a page."

Keep in mind that there is a wide range of picture books out there, from Eric Carle's *The Very Hungry Caterpillar* board book to Brian Selznick's Caldecott Medal–winning, five-hundred-page-plus book *The Invention of Hugo Cabret*. Picture books are for everybody, and all ages can enjoy them. If your adolescent loves picture books, that's fine. Illustrated books about political events and social movements can be great fodder for family discussions. But while picture books are wonderful, your adolescent also needs to consistently read chapter books at his or her current reading level.

Middle- and high-school teachers successfully use picture books to introduce historical events. *Henry's Freedom Box*, an award-winning picture book about a slave who escapes to freedom, can jump-start a class discussion about slavery and the Underground Railroad. Teachers can pair *Henry's Freedom Box* with a classic like Toni Morrison's *Beloved*, which is also about escaping from slavery. *The Man Who Walked Between the Towers* is a picture book that gives background information about the Twin Towers, and teachers may read it out loud to introduce the topic of 9/11.

What about chat fiction? My kids read stories in text format on the app Hooked. Is that as good as reading a novel?

Chat fiction started with the app Hooked, which was developed to tell six-minute horror stories via a series of text messages. Both Hooked and its competitor Yarn produce fiction that is read on a smartphone app, as if the reader is eavesdropping on a texted conversation. These apps are popular with adolescents. Hooked has been downloaded more than twenty million times.

Here's a sample from Hooked's website:

Ella: RU There? I'm in trouble.
Ella: Pls answer me.
Ella: Pls, Pls, Pls.
Jacob: I'm here. What's up? U ok?
Ella: No. I'm in serious trouble.

Since chat fiction is all conversation—and it's not exactly Newbery Medal–winning dialogue, it has little room for character development, setting, descriptions, or theme. It's clearly not as good as reading a well-written novel or article. And chat fiction is scary. At a recent sleepover party in my hometown, a Hooked story about a double murder, bloody blanket, and mysterious baby crying in the basement kept a group of twelve-year-old girls up until two in the morning. They were too frightened to go to sleep.

Before diving into the world of chat fiction, encourage your kids to pick up one of the exciting books that hook, discussed in an upcoming chapter.

Do kids have to stick with their reading level? What are teachers talking about when they mention Lexile reading levels?

Teachers like students to stick to their reading levels. It can be frustrating for kids to try to read up a level and find they don't understand what they are reading. In order for adolescents to experience flow, where they are so immersed in a book that they lose track of time and their surroundings, they need to be able to understand the author's words.

Many schools use Lexile levels to determine a student's reading ability. Your child may be tested in class and given a Lexile score. If your child receives a 550 L Lexile score, he or she will be assigned to read a book that is in the 550 L range. Books are given computer-generated Lexile scores, which are dependent on the book's readability. The higher the Lexile number, the more difficult the reading material.

Schools may also use computerized reading incentive programs such as Accelerated Reader (AR), Reading Counts, and other leveled programs that assign a number or a letter to your child based on his or her reading ability. After reading a book on the assigned level, the child takes a test on the computer about the book. Doing well on the tests means he or she can move up to higher-level books.

When my daughter was in elementary school, she came home one day and proudly announced that she scored an *F* in reading. An *F*? Before I rushed into the attic to dust off our old Bob Books for remedial readers, she mentioned that her goal was to be an *H*. And her friend Ella, who was reading chapter books in preschool, was already an *N*. It was helpful for me to get information about the reading program from her teacher during our parent-teacher conference, so I understood what my daughter was talking about.

If your child is given a numerical AR rating of 5.5, it means he or she is reading at a fifth-grade level at month five. (The first number represents grade level, and the second number is the month.) For more information on finding books based on your child's grade-level scores, go to Scholastic.com, which contains articles about leveled reading and book suggestions.

Since I want to simplify my life, I don't pay too much attention to Lexile and AR levels (unless my kid [or her teacher] tells me that she is struggling with the leveled reading). It's too complicated to keep track of all those changing numbers and letters, and I'm OK with my kids reading above or below their computer assigned levels. It's easier to go the library armed with four or five good book recommendations and check them all out. If my kids occasionally try to read a book that's too hard for them, then my husband, or I or a sibling, can help them. Or they could read along to the audiobook version of the book.

At a recent parent-teacher conference, my son's fifth-grade teacher mentioned that he needs to improve his reading-comprehension skills. My son does not have a learning difference, but he scored below the state average on a standardized test. How can I help him with reading comprehension?
First, ask his teacher for specific feedback. Which reading comprehension skills does your son need to improve? Making inferences? Identifying a theme? Summarizing the main idea of a passage? Identifying the author's purpose? (Or it could be a different concept.) Once you know where he needs help, ask the teacher for books or workbooks and suggestions. She may mention websites like IXL, which has

lessons and exercises based on state standardized tests, or a Spectrum Reading Workbook that you can purchase for about nine dollars.

When my daughter needed to work on her comprehension skills, it was effective to have her read out loud. (Reading out loud slows the reading process, so you can see if your child is skipping words.) When my daughter encountered an unfamiliar word or confusing sentence, she'd reread it. If she didn't understand after rereading, she'd read the next full paragraph, and then we'd discuss it. We also went over the comprehension questions found at the back of her leveled reading books.

My daughter likes to reread the same novel several times. Should I encourage her to try something new?

Our twelve-year-old neighbor read the *Harry Potter* series four times. He enjoyed it, and rereading books can increase comprehension skills. There are many adults who read their favorite novels every year or every few years. If a teen is a devoted reader who reads a wide variety of books, then occasionally rereading a book that he or she loves is fine.

But we learn more about the world and improve our vocabulary when we explore a variety of genres. Science-fiction books, like the young adult version of *The Martian*, feature words and concepts that you won't find in a teen murder mystery, such as *Hunting Jack the Ripper*. To get an adolescent to try a new genre or format, identify what elements he or she likes about a current favorite book. For example, if your daughter exclusively rereads a high-school romance, she may enjoy a dystopian novel, like Veronica Roth's *Divergent*, that also features teen love. If your son repeatedly reads a martial-arts comic, you could encourage him to try a chapter book like *Diary of a 6th Grade Ninja*, by Marcus Emerson.

In addition, see if your daughter is interested in Reading Without Walls, a reading challenge from Gene Luen Yang, author of popular graphic novels. On his website, Yang asks readers to

1. Read a book about a character who doesn't look like you or live like you. When you seek out books about people who are different from you, it opens up your world.
2. Read a book about a topic you don't know much about.
3. Read a book in a format that you don't normally read for fun. This might be a chapter book, a graphic novel, a poetry book, a picture book, or a hybrid book.

My son reads while lying on his back on the living room floor. Drake blares from his phone. How can he possibly concentrate on his book? Shouldn't he be sitting up in a chair, in a quiet room so he can focus?

As long as your kid is engaged in the book he's reading, it doesn't matter how or where he reads. It can be inside, outside, upright, lying down, in silence, or with Bruno Mars blasting. As I write this sentence, my youngest reads on the couch with our dog, Mickey, on her lap, licking her hand; Ed Sheeran croons; and she is miles away, immersed the dystopian world of Marie Lu's *Legend*.

How can you tell when your son is engaged in what he is reading? An engaged reader's eyes focus on the printed page. He does not check his cell phone. (Ideally, the cell phone is in a different room.) He may smile or chuckle while reading and pause to tell you what is happening, or share an unusual fact he just learned. Or he may ask you the definition of a word in the book. He can answer questions such as "What's happening in your book right now?" or "Which character do you like best, and why?"

If your son is a disengaged reader, he flips through the pages, checks his phone, stares into space, spins in his seat, or flops on the floor and talks to the dog. He has trouble answering basic questions about his book's plot and characters. Instead of inquiring about a challenging vocabulary word, your rapidly growing teen may ask questions completely unrelated to his novel. As he polishes off his second box of Clif bars with one hand and squints at the pages of his book, he wants to know, "What's for dinner?" "When *is* dinner?" and "Why can't we have dinner sooner?"

But if you have a disengaged reader, take heart; he can still become engaged, with the right reading material and by making reading the most interesting activity in the room. These topics will be addressed in upcoming chapters.

Is there any difference between reading on an e-reader or on a cell phone, versus reading a paperbound book?

Reading on an e-reader or cell phone can be just as good as reading a paperbound copy of a book *if* an adolescent does not get distracted by the games, social media, and embedded links that are on phones and e-readers. A book read on a cell phone or a tablet is one irresistible click away from *Carpool Karaoke* videos.

Kids with vision issues can make fonts bigger on their e-reader or phone, or can listen to an audiobook instead. Teens who read below grade level and English language learners appreciate the privacy and dictionaries e-readers and phones provide.

The following chart summarizes the pros and cons of e-readers.

E-books versus paper books	
Pros for e-books on cell phone, tablet, or iPad	**Pros for paper books**
Can instantly download books, so there is always something to read	No online distractions. Not competing against incoming Snapchats, texts, and tweets
Font can be enlarged for vision issues	Feel of book and turning the physical pages is more satisfying

Pros for e-books on cell phone, tablet, or iPad	Pros for paper books
Lightweight and easy portability to bring multiple books on vacation	Does not need to be charged
Quick dictionary lookup function (if they actually use this)	Does not have the annoying percentage done sign
Privacy: no one needs to know what they are reading	Does not emit light that makes it harder to sleep
Can listen to the book on Audible app	Does not have hyperlinks that can disrupt the flow or reading

There seems to be an app for everything these days. Is there one out there that can encourage my preteen to read for pleasure?
There are several apps that are designed to get kids and adults excited about reading. Whether they will work for emerging readers remains to be seen. Here is an overview of several of them:

- Bookout—Read More. With this app, adolescents can track the books they are reading as well as their thoughts and favorite quotes. With Bookout, users set reading goals and generate reading stats and cool infographics on things like reading speed. They can then share this information on social media. My youngest daughter likes this app, which also has a reading-reminder alarm that goes off daily.
- Reading Rewards. Preteens can track their reading on Reading Rewards, which offers incentive points. As adolescents log their reading, they can go up levels, earn badges, and accumulate reading reward miles, which can be redeemed for a joke of the day or used to purchase a reward from a parent.

- Freedom and similar apps turn off web access for up to eight hours. Your adolescent can set an Internet block for a certain number of minutes so that he or she can read undisturbed.

What makes screens more attractive to adolescents than reading a book? What can we do about it?

Research shows that technology is designed to hook us. Every time we get new information via social media, our brains produce the chemical dopamine. Dopamine tells our brains that we want more of whatever we just experienced. A hit of dopamine motivates animals (including people) to repeat behaviors. Dopamine is what drives lab rats to press a lever over and over again for food pellets. It also keeps us clicking on links and Facebook feeds.[5]

Friendships and socializing are important to adolescents, and for many of them, the majority of their socializing is done through their screens. Reading a novel is typically a solitary activity. Teens may view reading books as stealing time away from their friends.

Screens are here to stay. But we need to take breaks from them to interrupt the dopamine feed. If necessary, adolescents can psych themselves up for a tech timeout. Experts advise using Bob the Builder's question-and-answer technique: "Can I shut off my smartphone for two hours? Yes, yes, I can!"[6] (Repeat as necessary.) Or chant, "I am human, hear me ROAR! I won't be dope-fed anymore!" We are the boss of our screens. We decide when and for how long we will go on and offline.

It's OK to use our parental authority to tell kids to take a screen break. Adolescents can leave their phones at home when they walk the dog, go outside to ride a bike, go to the local pool, or go to a friend's house. Parents and kids, please turn off the phones at meals and when you are reading a good book. Put them in airplane mode when you go to the library, the bookstore, a performance, a sports practice, or any kind of meeting. Declare a screen-free weekend morning. You'll be surprised at how invigorating it feels.

Part 2
Carrying Out a Reading Project

Five

Introducing Reading for Pleasure and Selling Its Benefits

Our family reading project had two main objectives that I hoped to accomplish in the most enjoyable way possible (for all of us).

- Main goal: Teen and preteens read books for pleasure and eventually become self-motivated, independent readers. (Independent readers select their own books, keep track of what books they want to read next, and enjoy reading during their free time.) Once my kids enjoyed reading, I wanted to move from a reading manager to a consultant role as soon as possible.
- Secondary goal: increase reading of any long-form text, including but not limited to newspaper articles, magazines, blogs, concert reviews, and anything else with sequential sentences.

I didn't have a timeline for getting my kids interested in books again. It might take six weeks, six months, or a year or more. It would depend on the child—on his or her current interest or disinterest in reading, success in finding engaging reading material, and other factors. But the first step was to reintroduce my kids to the concept of reading for pleasure.

Introducing Reading for Pleasure

How we frame reading can persuade our adolescents to give books a chance. When you start a reading project, check out three to five books that could hook your adolescent. (See chapter 6 for the list of books that hook.) Don't drag your dormant or emerging reader into the young adult section of the library, where he or she may be overwhelmed by the hundreds of choices. While most of us love variety, studies show that we buy more products and services when the choice is limited.[1] Keep the three to five engaging books on hand but out of sight. To get your adolescent started down the path of reading, put good books directly in his or her hands. (As soon as children become engaged readers, they will be navigating the library on their own.)

Any vacation day or weekend morning when your adolescent is in a relaxed mood is a good time to discuss reading for pleasure. For example, you may want to start by asking your daughter, as she chomps on her favorite flavor of Cheerios, if she has heard of any good books lately. You could continue on to ask what her friends are currently reading.

If she responds with a title or several book titles, that's terrific. Seize the moment. Have her check the public-library website to determine if the books are available, put a hold on them, and then get the books into her hands as soon as possible. (For parents with bigger book budgets, your child can buy the book from Amazon or Barnes & Noble online or during a visit to a local bookstore.)

If you have a dormant or emerging adolescent reader, you may receive the following responses to the question "What book do you think you might like to read for fun?"

"Read for fun? I read enough books for school!" Short pause as she glances down at her buzzing smartphone. "Can you drive me and Jenna to the movies tonight?"

Or,

"Read? I don't need to read *more*." The subject is changed to a class where she is doing well without reading. "I just got a ninety-one on my chemistry test. I *never* read for that class."

Or,

"Read? I'm too busy to read! None of my friends read. Their parents don't make them." Exasperated huff. "You are stressing me out by even bringing this up!"

Fortunately, today's teens and preteens are smart. They can easily understand the research about the benefits of reading described earlier. Once your kid finds the right book, reading will sell itself. But when you are introducing reading for fun, it helps to "sell, not tell." Telling (lecturing) isn't as effective as having a conversation that helps your kids see the benefits of books.

Try to keep the discussion positive. Rather than telling your daughter that Snapchat causes brain atrophy and she is literally wasting her life away on social media, enumerate the importance of balancing reading with screens. Regale her with the reading benefits listed in the first chapter, and tailor them to her wants. Adolescents often like to know "What's in it for me?" before taking on a new project. If your daughter has expressed frustration with friend drama and wants an escape, the right book can give her one. Is her heart set on attending a highly ranked college? Reading widely increases SAT scores. Does your son desperately want to beat his friends in his Fantasy Football league? Point out books and podcasts that can give him tips and a competitive edge.

At this point in the discussion, if your adolescent has not fled from the room, you could bring up how reading comprehension is associated with future success in the workplace. When I mention this to a carpool of middle-school kids, one budding banker perked up and asked, "You mean reading more books means more money?" The car fell silent as they imagined dollar bills cascading from book spines.

Reading can help your adolescent meet his or her career goals. Does your daughter want to go into the medical field? Point out that reading and comprehending textbooks and research papers are crucial in nursing and medical schools. She dreams of being a pilot? The major airlines require that their pilots have a four-year college degree, preferably a bachelor of sciences, and that will also involve reading many long-form sentences. The more she reads now, the more stamina she will have for the two hundred to six hundred pages of weekly college reading.

After your discussion, hand over the three or four books that hook. Briefly, explain why these books could be a great read. If one is recommended by a "cool" cousin or aunt, be sure to mention it. Or point out if it's a YA book that has a movie or TV version coming out with one of your child's favorite actors.

One of the ways that reading experts get students to try a book is to make it a personal gift. The teacher hands the book to the student and says, "I read this, and I thought of you. Try it; you'll like it." If the student respects the teacher, he or she will give the book a shot. I've witnessed this technique work when a grandparent or a cousin places a book in the hands of one of my kids and explains why the book is a good match.

Teachers also hold book chats to get their students interested in reading. During a book chat, a teacher will hold up the latest John Green novel (for example) and enthusiastically read a few pages aloud or read the back cover. It's like a commercial for the book. My mother-in-law does minichats about a book before handing it to one of my children. Her enthusiasm about a novel encourages my kids to take the book out for a test ride.

Selling your adolescents on reading for pleasure is an ongoing conversation. That's because while a kid can fall in love with reading, he or she can also drop back into dormancy. When my kids get busy with homework and sports practices, they have less time and interest in books. My daughter disliked her assigned summer reading of Hawthorne's *The Scarlet Letter*, which led her back to complaining about the act of reading. Fortunately, she also decided to read Nicola Yoon's *Everything, Everything*, which swept her away. If your adolescent enjoyed reading once, she will again.

Building Confident Readers

Studies show that how kids label themselves can change their behavior.[2] Avoid announcing that "Jimmy is just not a reader" in front of your son. Once he starts reading anything—*ESPN Magazine* articles or Spiderman graphic novels—label him as a reader. Your son may start thinking of himself as one and acting upon it.

Dormant and emerging readers who struggle with finishing a long novel often prefer short hi-lo books and graphic novels. The length and visuals of graphic novels are less intimidating than full-length books. If your kid reads several graphic novels, tell him or her that *you* want to check out a graphic novel. Ask your child for a recommendation, and then read what he or she suggests. The more kids read and recommend books to others, the more confident they become about their abilities, and the more likely it is they will continue to read for pleasure.

Six

Finding the Right Book That Will Hook Your Adolescent

The Scholastic.com *Kids and Family Reading Report* (fifth edition) states, "Nearly three-quarters of both boys and girls (73%) say they would read more if they could find more books they like." *Finding the right book is key to getting an adolescent hooked on reading.* Reading experts, librarians, teachers, parents, and teens all confirm that the right book can unlock the gate to the land of loving reading. And it can unlock it quickly. But how does a teen find this magical right book?

Why people enjoy certain books and genres is a mystery. It may be a combination of our innate personality traits, experiences, mood, and stage in life. It's similar to how we select a favorite song, artist, or ice-cream flavor. We just know what we like when we experience it. Understanding why adolescents read can help you find the books that can hook them.

ADOLESCENTS READ TO ENJOY AND FIND MORE INFORMATION ABOUT THEIR CURRENT INTERESTS

Teachers advise "to meet your children where they are" (not where you want them to be). Help your adolescent select a book about one of his or her current interests or passions. Does your preteen love baseball or enjoy fashion? If so, get him or her a book on one of those topics.

Does this advice work? Yes, it does. I've witnessed preteens who love horseback riding gobble up the *Canterwood Crest* series, which is full of horses and girl drama. Kwame Alexander's *The Crossover*, about growing up on and off the basketball court, entrances basketball fans.

It also helps to build on the articles, comics, websites, and blogs that your teen currently enjoys. Here are examples of how this can work:

- An eleven-year-old Minecraft addict spends hours on the Minecraft website reading about the latest "killer builds." He also reads about a novel called *Diary of a Minecraft Zombie*, which is described on the website. During his next library visit, he picks it up and reads it in one day.
- A thirteen-year-old follows YouTube star Zoella's blog. Besides begging her mother for a Zoella-inspired haircut and dip dye, she also asks for Zoella's best-selling novel, *Girl Online*.
- A twelve-year-old basketball fanatic skims ESPN.com on a daily basis. During a school library visit, he is encouraged to check out a book. He remembers that ESPN.com mentioned Mike Lupica's book about basketball travel teams, and he checks it out from the school library.

- A fifteen-year-old reads *People* magazine, which features an article on hunky Liam Hemsworth, a star in *The Hunger Games* movie. She decides to read the entire Hunger Games series so she can continue to daydream about Liam Hemsworth.
- A thirteen-year-old receives Taylor Swift tickets for her birthday. She reads online concert reviews of the upcoming tour and asks for a Taylor Swift biography (which includes a giant signed poster). She reads the entire book in two nights.

Besides enjoying their current interests, adolescents also are motivated to read for the following reasons:

ADOLESCENTS READ TO ESCAPE AND EXPERIENCE EXCITING WORLDS

The escapist appeal and emotional tone of a novel can captivate an adolescent reader. Teens and preteens read to get away from the mundane routine of their daily lives. When reading *The Hunger Games* or *The Maze Runner*, adolescents enter an exciting and dangerous world where teens are powerful. For my daughter who loves to bake, the *Cupcake Diary* series was a light, fun read, but it couldn't compare to *Harry Potter,* which consumed her imagination for months. My niece, who is on a competitive travel soccer team, prefers to escape with James Patterson's fantasy *Maximum Ride* series rather than books about soccer.

ADOLESCENTS READ TO REAFFIRM THAT THEY ARE NOT ALONE

Have a problem or concern? Well, it's highly likely that someone else has faced your challenge and written a book about it. Teens and preteens read to discover they aren't alone in their struggles. It's comforting to kids with learning differences to read Lynda Hunt's uplifting novel *A Fish in a Tree*, where the main character learns to cope with dyslexia. Adoptees may relate to *A Long Way Home* due to Saroo

Brierley's desire to find his birth mother and his anxiety before meeting her.

ADOLESCENTS READ FOR COURAGE AND ENCOURAGEMENT

True stories about people overcoming insurmountable odds, like *Unbroken* or *The Boys Who Stood Up to Hitler*, can inspire adolescents. Fiction can also provide solace. Penny Kittle reports in *Book Love* that one of her seniors, named Jeremy, "lost both parents as a small child and is being raised by his grandparents. He told me that Harry Potter gives him hope that he will overcome his own isolation and sorrow."

ADOLESCENTS READ TO EXPERIENCE SOMETHING AUTHENTIC

We are surrounded by fake news, unreal "reality TV," Photoshopped Instagram shots, and Facebook "friends" we never see. It's no wonder that adolescents (and adults) read to experience something real. Good books don't fake it. (It's too hard to counterfeit feelings and experiences in writing for over two hundred pages.) Authors share what their characters really look like, think, and feel. Teens want to read books with the real language they speak and encounter issues they face.

ADOLESCENTS READ TO EXPERIENCE ROMANCE AND LOVE

Teens and preteens read to experience love. This can be romantic love from a handsome, sparkly vampire, as depicted in the Twilight series, or love for an autistic sibling like in Cynthia Lord's *Rules*.

ADOLESCENTS READ TO LAUGH

Books like the *Diary of a Wimpy Kid* series and *The Hitchhiker's Guide to the Galaxy* are funny. So are Terry Pratchett's and David Sedaris's books. Much of the required reading for middle and high school is serious literature depicting wars, the dust bowl, Stalinism, and death. Adolescents enjoy a respite from these heavy topics by consuming a humorous book.

ADOLESCENTS READ ABOUT A PERSON WHOM THEY ADMIRE AND WANT TO BE LIKE

Adolescents read memoirs and biographies to experience and understand the lives of famous people. A budding zoologist reads Jane Goodall's biography to learn what studying wildlife for ten hours a day in the bush entails. Tennis players who dream of the pro circuit can read Andre Agassi's *Open*.

ADOLESCENTS READ TO TRAVEL TO A DISTANT PLACE OR TIME

Readers of Deborah Ellis's *The Breadwinner* can experience what it is like to live in Afghanistan under the Taliban without leaving their couch. Or they can time travel back to Germany and Denmark during World War II when they read *The Boys Who Challenged Hitler*.

ADOLESCENTS READ TO SOLVE PROBLEMS OR ANSWER QUESTIONS

Self-help books like *A Smart Girl's Guide to Knowing What to Say* by Patti Criswell advise adolescents on how to tell a friend to stop talking behind your back and the best ways to stand up to a bully. National Geographic Kids books, such as *Why?: Over 1,111 Answers to Everything*, explain things like what is really inside a turtle's shell and why the Earth doesn't just float off into space.

How to Find the Magical "Right Book"

Besides building on my adolescents' current interests, book recommendations from friends and cousins are our number-one source of books that hook. When you get a suggestion, have your adolescent keep track of it, and try to get the book as soon as possible. The following is a list of resources:

- Book recommendations from friends, teammates, older siblings, and cousins are one of the best sources of books that hook. One of my nieces is a devoted reader; she frequently passes on books and recommendations to my kids. Devoted readers love to share their favorite stories and can be a powerful reading influence. My nephews enjoyed the musical *Hamilton* and sent my daughter, who is also a *Hamilton* fan, a DK Eyewitness American Revolution book for her birthday. Ask your kids: Did anyone mention a book they love during language-arts class? What books are your friends and classmates consuming during sustained silent reading? When driving a bunch of kids to soccer practice every week, bring up the subject of their favorite books. If you are hanging out at endless baseball games with other parents, ask about what their children like to read.

- Grandparents, aunts and uncles, and family friends can give books that they enjoyed reading to your kids. My ten-year-old daughter loved Enid Blyton's the *Naughtiest Girl* series, which my mom gave her and read to her. She also enjoyed *A Dog's Purpose*, by W. Bruce Cameron, which my mother-in-law read for her book club and shared.

- Popular books that contain mature content that you don't want your adolescent to read are always a big draw. Once I admitted that I thought *The Hunger Games*, which depicts kids killing each other, might be too violent for my sixth grader, she immediately wanted to check it out of the library.

- A book that has been on the young adult and middle-school bestseller lists for over ten weeks. The *New York Times* has a weekly young adult hardcover bestseller list and a children's middle-grade list (https://www.nytimes.com/books/best-sellers).

- A book that your adolescent loves as a movie, TV show, or video game.
- Books that have buzz. These are the books the kids are arguing about on the school bus or talking about at lunch. Often, they are made into movies.
- Leverage teachers' book chats and books that they read out loud or assigned to the class. If your son loved Jerry Spinelli's *Maniac Magee* when his teacher read it, check out another book by Spinelli, such as *Stargirl*.
- Goodreads' read-alikes book lists. Anytime your child enjoys a book, you can find a similar book he or she may enjoy on Goodreads.com.
- The books that hook listed next. These are the engaging books that adolescents love. Many are the first book in a series. The beauty of a series is that the familiar characters and settings make it easier for an emerging reader to understand and enjoy the story. And your kid knows what book he or she is going to read next; he or she's on reading autopilot.

The more kids read, the easier and more enjoyable reading becomes. After finishing the approximately four thousand pages of the *Harry Potter* series, an adolescent gains confidence in his abilities. And he should. It's an accomplishment.

The List of Popular Books That Hook Teen and Preteen Readers

Books that hook don't have to be great literature, but they do have to be books that kids don't want to put down. The following list details the books that librarians, teachers, and parents report engage kids. Adolescents have also confirmed that they love these books. If you see a hardcover and paperback version of the book in the library, always check out the one with the newer, more modern, edgier cover.

Age Ten and Up: Realistic Fiction

- *Wonder*, by R. J. Palacio. A ten-year-old boy with a facial deformity enters a new school.
- *The One and Only Ivan*, by Katherine Applegate. Based on a true story of a gorilla named Ivan who lived behind a glass window in a shopping mall. When a baby elephant named Ruby arrives from the wild, Ivan starts to see his captivity in a different light.
- *Holes*, by Louis Sachar. Stanley Yelnats is sent to a boys' detention center, where the boys are forced to spend all day digging five-foot-by-five-foot holes. What is the warden searching for?
- *A Fish in a Tree*, by Lynda Hunt. A girl hides her dyslexia until a teacher helps her overcome her learning differences.
- *Out of My Mind*, by Sharon M. Draper. An eleven-year-old girl with cerebral palsy longs for a way to speak to her family and classmates.
- *The Wild Robot*, by Peter Brown. Roz the robot washes ashore onto a remote island with unfriendly inhabitants.
- *Esperanza Rising*, by Pam Munoz Ryan. A tragedy forces Esperanza to flee to California during the Great Depression and settle in a camp for Mexican farmworkers.
- *Because of Mr. Terupt*, by Rob B. Buyea. Mr. Terupt, a new, energetic fifth-grade teacher at Snow Hill School, relates to his students and makes learning fun until an accident changes everything.

- *Al Capone Does My Shirts* and its sequels, by Gennifer Choldenko. The adventures of a twelve-year-old who moves with his family to Alcatraz Island, where his dad works as a prison guard.
- *Million-Dollar Throw*, by Mike Lupica. Nate Brodie wins the chance to throw a pass through a target at a Patriots game for $1 million.
- *Smile*, by Raina Telgemeier (graphic novel). A sixth grader struggles with dental issues and with friends who turn out not to be so friendly.
- *Hatchet*, by Gary Paulsen. After a plane crash, thirteen-year-old Brian Robeson finds himself alone in the Canadian wilderness.
- Middle School, the Worst Year of My Life series, by James Patterson. Sixth grader Rafe Khatchadorian tries to break every rule in his school's oppressive code of conduct.
- *Rules*, by Cynthia Lord. Twelve-year-old Katherine just wants to be normal, but contends with a family life that revolves around her younger, autistic brother.
- *Princess Diaries* series, by Meg Cabot. A ninth grader living in a New York City loft is shocked to learn that she is the heir to a tiny European kingdom.
- *Princess Academy* series, by Shannon Hale. A group of girls are taken from their village to the palace so that the prince may select among them for a wife.
- *The Crossover*, by Kwame Alexander (free verse). Twins must come to terms with growing up on and off the basketball court.
- *Because of Winn-Dixie*, by Kate DiCamillo. A lonely ten-year-old named Opal adopts an orphaned dog whom she names Winn-Dixie, after the supermarket where he was found.

AGE TEN AND UP: HUMOROUS FICTION

- *Diary of a Wimpy Kid* series, by Jeff Kinney. Comical adventures and struggles of middle-school student Greg Heffley.
- *Max Crumbly* series, by Rachel Renée Russell. Middle schooler Max Crumbly faces down bullies and retrieves his father's comic book from the hands of thieves.
- *Timmy Failure: Mistakes Were Made*, by Stephen Pastis (graphic novel). A comically self-confident eleven-year-old boy believes he is a detective.
- *Big Nate* series, by Lincoln Pierce. The misadventures of Nate Wright, a spirited and rebellious sixth grader.
- *Gangsta Granny*, by David Walliams. Eleven-year-old Ben thinks his granny is boring until he learns about her criminal past.
- *Dork Diaries* series, by Rachel Renée Russell. Humorous diary of Nikki Maxwell, a fourteen-year-old girl who experiences the highs and lows of middle school.
- *My Weird School* series, by Dan Gutman. AJ and friends encounter wacky, wild, and weird teachers.
- *I Funny* and its sequels, by James Patterson. Jamie Grimm, a middle schooler who uses a wheelchair, hopes to make it big as the world's first sit-down comic.
- *Matilda*, by Roald Dahl. Matilda is an exceptional girl, but her parents and kid-hating headmistress think she's annoying.
- *Diary of a 6th Grade Ninja*, by Marcus Emerson. Chase, a scrawny new kid at school, is excited when he is invited to join a secret group of sixth-grade ninjas.
- Joke books for aspiring comedians, like *Jokelopedia*, by Eva Blank.

AGE TEN AND UP: ACTION AND ADVENTURE AND FANTASY

- *Harry Potter* series, by J. K. Rowling. The adventures of a boy wizard and his friends.
- *The Lightning Thief* (the first of the Percy Jackson series), by Rick Riordan. Twelve-year-old Percy Jackson tries to save humanity from a thief who has stolen Zeus's thunderbolt.
- *Fablehaven* series, by Brandon Mull. A brother and sister discover their grandparents run a haven for magical creatures.
- *Artemis Fowl* series, by Eoin Colfer. Twelve-year-old Artemis, a millionaire and criminal mastermind, plots to kidnap a dangerous fairy.
- *The False Prince*, by Jennifer Neilson. This first book in a trilogy centers around Sage, an orphan who is forced into a competition to become a prince.
- *The Isle of the Lost: A Decendents Novel*, by Melissa de la Cruz. Disney villains and their offspring are exiled to an island where they plan to bring back magic and free themselves.
- Inkheart trilogy, by Cornelia Funke. The adventures of Meggie Folchart, a teen who has the ability to bring characters from books to life.
- *Escape from Mr. Lemoncello's Library* and its sequels, by Chris Grabenstein. A group of twelve-year-olds are locked into a futuristic library and must find their way out.
- Chronicles of Narnia, by C. S. Lewis. Four siblings enter the world of Narnia, a once-peaceful land inhabited by dwarfs and talking beasts that has been turned into eternal winter by the White Witch.
- *Kingdom Keepers: Disney After Dark*, by Ridley Pearson. Five teens work as holographic-theme-park hosts by day, and by night, they battle the Disney villains.

- The *Warriors* series, by Erin Hunger. A complex society of cats, filled with rulers, warriors, healers, and hunters, is disrupted.
- *A Series of Unfortunate Events*, by Lemony Snicket. After their parents' death, three orphaned siblings are placed in the custody of a violent relative, Count Olaf, who tries to steal their inheritance.
- *The Graveyard Book*, by Neil Gaiman. A boy, who escapes the mysterious murder of his birth family, is taken in by the ghosts at the local graveyard.
- *I Survived the Sinking of the* Titanic, by Lauren Tarshis. A ten-year-old boy describes the sinking of the *Titanic*.
- *The Invention of Hugo Cabret*, by Brian Selznick (part graphic novel). A twelve-year-old orphan secretly lives in a Paris train station.
- Amulet series, by Kazu Kibuishi (graphic novel). A brother and sister try to save their mother, who is taken to an underground world inhabited by demons, robots, and talking animals.
- *Bone*, by Jeff Smith (graphic novel). Fantasy-adventure story of three misfit cousins who are run out of Boneville and find themselves lost in a land of dragons and evil forces.

AGE TEN AND UP: NONFICTION

- *Who Was Martin Luther King Jr.?*, by Bonnie Bader, and *Who Was Albert Einstein?*, by Jess Brallier. Engaging series of biographies.
- *How They Croaked: The Awful Ends of the Awfully Famous*, by Georgia Bragg. Describes how nineteen world figures died. Readers will feel lucky to live in a world with antibiotics and 9-1-1.
- *Weird but True* series, by National Geographic Kids. Outrageous facts paired with interesting visuals.

- *Horrible History* series, by Terry Deary. An engaging look at history includes gory details of wars and conflicts.
- *Home of the Brave*, by Katherine Applegate. A refugee from Africa comes to America; he sees snow for the first time and slowly makes friends.
- *The Notorious Benedict Arnold*, by Steven Sheinkin. The fast-paced story of one of America's most notorious traitors, who was also one of our greatest patriots.
- Uncle John's Bathroom Series, by Bathroom Readers' Institute. These books contain weird facts, odd news, strange science and information on things like how to give your dog CPR and how to start your own country.
- *Hidden Figures*, by Margot Lee Shetterly (young readers edition). The true story of the black female mathematicians who helped build the NASA field center at Langley.
- *The Big Book of Why*, by the editors of *Sports Illustrated Kids*. Answers sports-specific questions.
- *Bomb: The Race to Build—and Steal—the World's Most Dangerous Weapon*, by Steve Sheinkin. The story of the plotting, the risk-taking, and deceit that created the atomic bomb.

AGE TWELVE AND UP: ACTION/FANTASY FICTION

- The Hunger Games series, by Suzanne Collins. Katniss Everdeen takes her younger sister's place in the Hunger Games, a televised competition in which teenagers are chosen at random to fight to the death.
- The Divergent series, by Veronica Roth. In a world where people are divided into factions based on human virtues,

Tris Prior is warned she will never fit into any of the groups.
- *Savvy*, by Ingrid Law. Twelve-year-old Mibs can't wait to turn thirteen, which is the age when she will receive a supernatural power, known as a "savvy."
- The Selection series, by Kiera Cass. Thirty-five girls compete for the heart of a handsome prince.
- The *Alex Rider* series, by Anthony Horowitz. A teenager is recruited to be a spy by the British intelligence agency after learning secrets about his uncle's life.
- The *Maximum Ride* series, by James Patterson. Genetically enhanced kids who can fly are on the run from part-human, part-wolf predators.
- *City of Bones* (the first book in the Mortal Instruments series), by Cassandra Clare. Teenager Clary gets drawn into the world of the Shadowhunters, teens who kill demons and monsters.
- The *Lord of the Rings* trilogy, by J. R. Tolkien. The future of civilization rests in the power of the One Ring, which ends up in the hands of a young hobbit.
- The *Ranger's Apprentice* series, by John Flanagan. Fifteen-year-old Will is chosen as an apprentice to the Rangers, who protect the kingdom.
- *Journey to Star Wars: The Force Awakens Lost Stars*, by Claudia Gray. Two childhood friends grow up to be an Imperial officer and a Rebel pilot and must fight against each other.
- *The Maze Runner* (and its sequels and prequels), by James Dashner. Thomas wakes up to find his memory erased and is welcomed by boys whose memories are also gone. The only way out of his new home is through a treacherous maze.

- *I Am Number Four*, by Pittacus Lore. Teenage aliens with superpowers fight an army of xenoforms responsible for massacring their entire planet.
- Twilight series, by Stephenie Meyer. High-school student Bella enters into a dangerous romance with Edward, a handsome vampire.

AGE TWELVE AND UP: REALISTIC AND HISTORICAL FICTION

- *Crash*, by Jerry Spinelli. Crash Coogan transforms from smug jock into an empathetic person.
- *A Night Divided*, by Jennifer Nielsen. A twelve-year-old whose family is divided by the Berlin Wall takes a dangerous chance to reach freedom.
- *El Deafo*, by Cece Bell (graphic novel). The author chronicles her experiences navigating school while wearing an unwieldy hearing aid.
- *Small Steps*, by Louis Sacher. Two years after being released from a juvenile-correction center, Armpit is home in Texas and trying to straighten out his life.
- *The Sisterhood of the Traveling Pants*, by Ann Brashares. Four best friends stay connected over the summer break through a pair of jeans they take turns sharing.
- *Hoot*, by Carl Hiaasen: An ecological mystery made up of endangered miniature owls and the owls' unlikely allies— three middle-school kids.
- *Ghost*, by Jason Reynolds. "Ghost" Cranshaw has been running ever since the night his father shot a gun at him and his mother. Ghost can join an elite track team, as long as he stops getting into fights at school.
- *American Born Chinese*, by Gene Luen Yang (graphic novel). Jin Wang starts at a new school where he's the only Chinese-American student.

- *The Book Thief*, by Markus Zusak. Liesel is sent to live with a foster family in World War II Germany. She learns to read with help from her new family and Max, a Jewish refugee whom they are hiding under the stairs.

AGE TWELVE AND UP: MEMOIR/BIOGRAPHY

- *Unbroken* (young adult version), by Laura Hillenbrand. After a plane crash during World War II, Olympian Louis Zamperini spends forty-seven days in a raft before he's caught by the Japanese Navy.
- *A Long Walk to Water*, by Linda Soo Park. The story of two Sudanese twelve-year-olds struggling for survival.
- *A Long Way Gone*, by Ishmael Beah. The true story of Ishmael Beah, who becomes an unwilling boy soldier during a civil war in Sierra Leone.
- *I Am Malala: How One Girl Stood Up for Education and Changed the World* (young readers edition), by Malala Yousafzai and Patricia McCormick. A Nobel Peace Prize winner retells her experiences at home and at school in Pakistan.
- *Shoe Dog*, by Phil Knight (young adult version). Story of how the founder of Nike built his multibillion-dollar business.
- *The Boys Who Challenged Hitler*, by Phillip Hoose. A Danish fifteen-year-old, his brother, and a handful of schoolmates resolve to take action against the Nazis.
- *The Absolutely True Diary of a Part-Time Indian*, by Sherman Alexie. Junior leaves his school on the Spokane Indian reservation to attend an all-white high school.
- *A Long Way Home*, by Saroo Brierley. Five-year-old Saroo gets lost thousands of miles away from his Indian village and must learn to survive.

AGE FOURTEEN (GRADE 9) AND UP: REALISTIC FICTION/ RELATIONSHIPS

- *The Fault in Our Stars*, by John Green. A sixteen-year-old cancer patient meets and falls in love with a member of her cancer support group.
- *Everything, Everything*, by Nicola Yoon. Because of extreme allergies, Maddie has not left her house for seventeen years, until a handsome boy moves in next door.
- *The Sun Is Not a Star*, by Nicola Yoon. When Natasha, who is twelve hours away from being deported to Jamaica, and Daniel keep running into each other in New York City, could it be fate pushing them together?
- *The Perks of Being a Wallflower*, by Stephen Chbosky. A high-school freshman is rescued from bleak loneliness by a group of friendly misfits.
- *The Hate U Give*, by Angie Thomas. Starr Carter is with her friend when he is shot and killed by the police. She is the only eyewitness and must decide how much to reveal about what she saw.
- *Eleanor and Park*, by Rainbow Rowell. The story of two star-crossed misfits who fall in love.
- *A Dog's Purpose*, by W. Bruce Cameron. The emotional, and at times funny, story of a dog's many lives.
- *Looking for Alaska*, by John Green. Miles is sent to boarding school, where he meets the enchanting and wild Alaska Young.
- *Anna and the French Kiss*, by Stephanie Perkins. Anna is not happy about spending her senior year at a Paris boarding school. Complications arise when she develops feelings for a classmate.
- *To All the Boys I Loved Before,* by Jenny Han. Lara Jean pens never-to-be-mailed letters to every boy she's ever liked. But the letters are accidently sent out.

- *Perfect Chemistry*, by Simone Elkeles. A romance between two unlikely lab partners: Brittany, the school's "golden girl," and Alex, a member of a Latino Bloods gang.
- *The Truth about Forever*, by Sarah Dessen. Macy bottles up her grief over her father's death, keeping a flawless facade of good grades until she meets handsome Wes.
- *Speak,* by Laurie Halse Anderson. A freshman high school student refuses to speak ever since she called the cops on summer party, where she was sexually assaulted.
- *Aristotle and Dante Discover the Secrets of the Universe,* by Benjamin Alire Sáenz. Two fifteen-year-old boys become unlikely friends and explore issues surrounding their sexuality.
- *Dear Martin*, by Nic Stone. Seventeen-year-old Justyce McAllister, a scholar-athlete, is roughed up by the police and wonders if he will always be judged by the color of his skin.
- *Milk and Honey*, by Rupi Kaur. Poems about love and loss.

Age Fourteen (Grade 9) and Up: Mystery/Action

- *The Curious Incident of the Dog in the Night-Time*, by Mark Haddon. A fifteen-year-old boy who lives with his father, loves animals, and doesn't understand human emotions investigates the murder of a neighbor's dog.
- *The Da Vinci Code*, by Dan Brown. A murder in the Louvre museum reveals a sinister plot to uncover a secret that has been protected by a secret society.
- *One of Us Is Lying*, by Karen McManus. Four high-profile classmates are suspects in a fellow student's murder.
- *Shelter*, by Harlan Coben. When Mickey Bolitar's new girlfriend vanishes, Mickey follows her trail into a dark underworld and learns about a shocking conspiracy.

- *The Fixer,* by Jennifer Lynn Barnes. Tess is thrust into a world of dangerous intrigue when she is forced to move to Washington, DC, to live with a sister she hasn't talked to in years.
- *Six of Crows,* Leigh Bardugo. In this fantasy thriller, six teens with various powers come together to break into a prison and retrieve a hostage.

AGE FOURTEEN (GRADE 9) AND UP: DYSTOPIAN/FANTASY/SCIENCE FICTION

- *The 5th Wave,* by Rick Yancy. After a series of alien attacks destroy our planet, a teenager searches for her brother and forms an alliance with a mysterious young man.
- *Lady Midnight,* by Cassandra Clare. Emma Carstairs grows into a woman determined to discover who killed her parents.
- Legend trilogy, by Marie Lu. June, born into an elite family in the Futuristic Republic, searches for a renowned criminal in order to avenge her brother's death.
- *Matched,* by Ally Condie. In Cassia's world, the government controls everything and "matches" people to their mates.
- *Gone,* by Michael Grant. After everyone over the age of fifteen disappears from a small California town, the teenagers left behind grow strange mutant powers.
- *Ready Player One,* by Ernest Cline. Set in 2044, reality is an ugly place where people spend all their time plugged into a virtual utopian world trying to figure out clues left by its creator. Whoever finds all three clues inherits incredible wealth.
- *Cinder,* by Marissa Meyer. Cinder, a cyborg hated by her stepmother, becomes involved with a handsome prince.
- *Daughter of Smoke & Bone,* by Laini Taylor. 17-year-old Karou is an art student-who bounces between the human world and the family of mysterious creatures who raised her.

- *The Martian*, by Andy Weir (get the classroom edition, which doesn't have pages of technical information). Mark Watney finds himself stranded alone on Mars with no way to even signal Earth that he's alive.
- *The Way of Kings*, by Brandon Sanderson. Fantasy saga about magic, war, and the quest for power.
- *The Hitchhiker's Guide to the Galaxy*, by Douglas Adams. In this humorous science-fiction novel, Arthur Dent travels the galaxy getting into horrible messes and generally wreaking havoc.
- *American Gods*, by Neil Gaiman. Shadow, recently widowed and released from prison, becomes involved in a battle between the old gods of the immigrants and today's new gods, which are credit cards, TV, and the Internet.
- *Scythe*, by Neal Shusterman. In a world with no hunger, no disease, and no war, Scythes are the only ones who can end human life and keep the population under control. Two teens are chosen to apprentice to a scythe—a role that neither wants.
- *Jurassic Park*, by Michael Crichton. Things go terribly wrong at a dinosaur island theme park.

AGE FOURTEEN (GRADE 9) AND UP: NONFICTION

- *Black Hawk Down*, by Mark Bowden. The story of the 1993 mission where about a hundred elite US soldiers were dropped by helicopter into a teeming market in the heart of Somalia.
- *Chasing Lincoln's Killer*, by James L. Swanson. Account of the chase for Abraham Lincoln's assassin.
- *The Glass Castle*, by Jeannette Walls. The author tells of her experience growing up in a dysfunctional family of nonconformists.

- *Beneath a Scarlet Sky*, by Mark Sullivan. Fast-paced true story about a seventeen-year-old living during the Nazi occupation of Italy.
- *Stiff*, by Mary Roach. An account of what happens to our bodies postmortem.
- *The Girl with Seven Names*, by Hyeonseo Lee. A girl describes her harrowing escape from North Korea.
- *The Nazi Hunters: How a Team of Spies and Survivors Captured the World's Most Notorious Nazi*, by Neal Bascomb. The true story of a group of Jewish men brought together to capture and bring to justice a notorious Nazi war criminal.
- *The Finest Hours* (young readers edition), by Michael J. Touglas. The story of the shipwreck of two oil tankers and the dramatic coast guard rescue.
- *The Warrior's Heart*, by Eric Greitens (young adult adaptation). A former navy SEAL describes his journey from aiding victims of violence to protecting and serving people.
- *Miracle in the Andes: 72 Days on the Mountain and My Long Trek Home*, by Nando Parrado. Nando Parrado was unconscious for three days before he woke to find that the plane he was on had crashed into the Andes Mountains.

AGE SIXTEEN AND UP

- *A Court of Thorns and Roses*, by Sarah J. Maas (fantasy). When huntress Feyre kills a wolf, a beast-like creature demands retribution and drags her into a dangerous magical land.
- *Me Talk Pretty One Day*, by David Sedaris (humorous memoir). Stories about the author's eccentric family life.
- *Tell Me Three Things*, by Julie Buxbaum (contemporary YA). Jessie's dad remarries, they move from Chicago to Los Angeles, and she starts at a prep school where she feels like an outsider.

- *Wild*, by Cheryl Strayed (memoir). In the wake of her mother's devastating death, Cheryl Strayed decides to hike one thousand miles of the Pacific Crest Trail.
- *It* or *The Shining* or *The Stand* by Stephen King (horror): For teens who like to be terrified; these books are absorbing and scary.
- *Lonesome Dove*, by Larry McMurtry (fiction). Two ex–Texas Rangers lead a cattle drive from Texas to Montana and encounter heroes and outlaws, Indians and settlers, and lady love interests. Once teens get past the first thirty pages and the cowboys start their journey, they will be immersed in the story.
- *Water for Elephants*, by Sara Gruen (fiction). Jacob, a poor veterinary-school student, takes a job with a second-rate traveling circus. He falls in love with Marlena, the star performer.
- The If I Stay series, by Gail Forman (fiction). Mia is in a coma after a horrible car accident that kills the rest of her family; she struggles to decide if she wants to live.
- *Me before You*, by Jojo Moyes (fiction). Plucky Louisa Clark becomes a caregiver to a wealthy young banker left paralyzed from an accident.
- *All the Light We Cannot See*, by Anthony Doerr (fiction). The story of a blind French girl and a Nazi youth, set in World War II before the invasion of Paris.
- *Mr. Mercedes* (part of the Bill Hodges trilogy), by Stephen King (mystery thriller). Retired detective Bill Hodges tries to track down the Mercedes Killer, who ran down twenty-three people with a stolen car.
- The Game of Thrones series, by George R. R. Martin (fantasy). The royal Stark family must contend with the plotting Lannisters, frozen zombies, and other challenges.

- The *Jack Reacher* series, by Lee Child (thriller). After leaving the military police, Jack Reacher drifts around the United States investigating dangerous crimes.
- *Open*, by Andre Agassi (memoir). Honest and at times inspiring autobiography that describes how Agassi was painfully pushed into the world of tennis stardom by his ambitious father.
- *Pillars of the Earth*, by Ken Follett (historical fiction). Intergenerational epic story about the building of a cathedral in twelfth-century England.
- *Hellhound on His Trail*, by Hampton Sides (nonfiction thriller). Fast-paced, nonfiction thriller about the hunt for the man shot Martin Luther King Jr.
- *Wool*, by Hugh Howley (science fiction). In a future dystopian land, a community of men and women live in a giant silo underground, hundreds of stories deep. The society is full of regulations they believe are meant to protect them.

Note: The books most often cited for revitalizing reading in adolescents are the seven books in the *Harry Potter* series. Rick Riordan's various series about demigods and the Hunger Games series were also frequently credited.

HIGH-LO READS

As mentioned earlier, high-interest books with lower-level vocabulary and lower page counts can entice reluctant readers. If your teen is having trouble getting started, offer to read five pages for every three pages that he or she reads. Here are some engaging high-lo series:

- The *Alex Rider* series, by Anthony Horowitz. Fourteen-year-old Alex Rider discovers that his uncle and guardian has been murdered and is then sucked into his uncle's undercover world.

- *Shelter* (part of the Mickey Bolitar series), by Harlan Coben. When Mickey Bolitar's new girlfriend vanishes, he follows her trail into a dark underworld and learns about a shocking conspiracy.
- The Michael Vey series, by Richard Paul Evans. An under-sized ninth-grade boy dealing with Tourette's syndrome learns he has the superpower to electrify people.
- *The Recruit*, part of the Cherub series, by Robert Muchamore. Twelve-year-old James is recruited to spy for the British Intelligence Service (called Cherub).
- *Airborn*, by Kenneth Oppel. The adventures of Matt Cruse, a cabin boy aboard the airship *Aurora*, who encounters mystical beings and dangerous sky pirates.
- The Matched series, by Ally Condie. Cassia, a model student and daughter, lives in a society that chooses her mate. What if they make the wrong choice?
- The Legend series, by Marie Lu. Fifteen-year-old June is groomed for success in the Republic's elite military until her path crosses with fifteen-year-old Day, the country's most-wanted criminal.
- Graphic novels such as *Bone*, by Jeff Smith, and Raina Telgemeier's *Ghost* or *Drama*.
- *Treaties, Trenches, Mud, and Blood*, by Nathan Hale (graphic novel). Interesting and easy-to-understand true-life tales from World War I.

Magazines That Adolescents Enjoy

Take your adolescent to the library or bookstore to check out the magazine selection. When your kid finds one he or she likes, look for subscription deals online. (Also, grandparents often enjoy giving magazine subscriptions as birthday presents.) If you are waiting around at an airport or train station, encourage your kid to buy a magazine to peruse while traveling.

Here are some of the most popular magazines for adolescents (you may want to review a copy first to determine if it's appropriate for your preteen):

- *New Moon Girls* (articles are all written by girls ages eight to fourteen)
- *Seventeen*
- *Girls' Life*
- *Rolling Stone*
- *Sports Illustrated* (You can request to skip the Swimsuit Issue and get an extra free, regular issue instead.)
- *ESPN the Magazine*
- *Skateboarder* magazine
- *Ebony* magazine
- *Motor Trend*
- *People* magazine
- *Entertainment Weekly*
- *National Geographic*
- *Latina* magazine
- *Newsweek*
- *Time*
- *Popular Science*

This past summer, I ordered *Sports Illustrated* for my thirteen-year-old son. He consumed the first issue—including articles on golf, one of the world's least interesting sports—in one sitting. Since *Sports Illustrated* was a hit, I ordered *National Geographic*. *National*

Geographic reboots our family dinner conversations. If my kids are arguing relentlessly about who permanently borrowed my husband's earbuds, I whip out the *National Geographic* and redirect the conversation by reading aloud a few paragraphs of an article. In the June 2017 issue, I read aloud, and we discussed articles about

- a former photographer who renders textured 3-D models of famous artwork so blind people can feel the paintings they are unable to see;
- how holograms of the human body are used in anatomy classes;
- the struggles of people with albinism around the world; and
- how and why chimps find bright red faces more alluring than pale pink faces.

We had some good conversations on these topics.

Seven

Access to Books and Making Reading the Most Interesting Activity in the Room

No matter the country, children who come from homes containing the most print—newspapers, books, and magazines—have the highest reading scores.

—Jim Trelease[1]

Easy access to engaging reading material and flooding adolescents with books encourages them to read. We need plenty of books, magazines, and newspapers to flow into our home on a regular basis. Your kid may whip through an entire graphic novel in an afternoon or rapidly abandon three of the library books he or she selected. You need an adequate amount of reading material constantly available.

Reading specialist Jim Trelease suggests that parents follow the rule of the "Three B's." There should be books in the bedrooms, books in the bathrooms, and books at the breakfast table. These books (and magazines and graphic novels) need to be engaging, visible, and accessible.

If you are a neatnik or concerned that the Three B's will ruin the fêng shui of your home, try to reframe your thoughts. Reading material is not clutter. It's the essential ingredient for developing a reader. So sorry, Marie Kondo and all other organizational gurus out there, but rather than tidying up and moving entire bookcases into our closets, we *want* our books to obstruct our adolescents' views.

After reading this suggestion, I scattered graphic novels, magazines, and short books around the house. I left reading material on the couches, kitchen table, and beds. (But I skipped the bathroom, which is a temporary hideout for some of my family members.) Seeding the house with engaging reading material works. I found my adolescents perusing articles and graphic novels at the breakfast table and in their rooms.

Where to Get Books, Magazines, and Graphic Novels

Here are some suggestions for acquiring enough reading material to cover the Three B's:

- *Public libraries.* Local public libraries are the best source for free books, e-books, audiobooks, graphic novels, and magazines, among other reading materials. Many libraries have online catalogs where kids can reserve a book and find read-alikes or similar books. Libraries also have sales where you can purchase books, audiobooks, and graphic novels at reasonable prices.

    Before hitting the library, have your adolescent think of three authors that he or she wants to read, because some popular books may be checked out. You could also review the library's online catalog from home to see what's available and put holds on books that aren't.

At our library, patrons can check out up to twenty-five books per library card. People drag rolling carts and luggage carriers and load up, so if there is a book that your child might be interested in, remember, "If in doubt, check it out." The more books you have, the better.

When your adolescent is speeding through the first book in a trilogy, check out the next book so it's ready to go. (Keep up that reading momentum!) If your daughter likes her current book and it's not part of a series, check out two more books from the same author. Or search goodreads.com to find similar books.

- *Teacher classroom libraries and school libraries.* Language-arts, science, and history teachers may keep stacks of engaging books in their rooms for kids to borrow. School libraries are also a good source of books.
- *Thrift stores.* Many Goodwill stores sell books online as well as in their physical stores. Teens enjoy "thrifting," where they buy recycled T-shirts and hoodies. Have them browse the book section while they are there. Thrift stores may also sell magazines.
- *Garage sales*
- *Local independent bookstores, used bookstores, and chains like Barnes & Noble*
- *Online retailers like Amazon and Barnes & Noble*
- *BookBub* sends e-mail alerts of e-books that are available for $1.99, 99¢, or free. The e-mails match your interests, and you can request to only see certain book categories like young adult, bestsellers, or thrillers.
- *Friends and family.* Swap books back and forth with cousins, grandparents, and friends.

Make Reading the Most Interesting and Accessible Activity in the Room

Around age twelve, many children start to spend spans of time in their bedroom with the door firmly closed. While they emerge for food, rides, and money, they enjoy the privacy of their bedroom. *Make reading a book the most accessible and interesting thing in their room.* You can do this by taking the following steps:

- Remove the TV, iPad, desktop computer, and any other screen from your adolescent's bedroom, and put them in another room in the house. This will not make us popular, but we aren't running for mayor. (It's time to use the selective-hearing skills we developed when *we* were teens.) After moving through short stages of denial, anger, and bargaining, adolescents will reach acceptance and become accustomed to going to the family room to use the computer or watch TV.

- Move at least three books that hook into their bedroom and place them near the bed or near a chair. Your kids can decide on the most comfortable place to read.

- Make sure there are a reading-wedge pillow and a reading lamp that can easily be turned off while lying in bed. Also, some kids with learning differences like ADHD focus better on reading if they can have something to fiddle with, such as a stress ball. If this is true for your child, then have stress balls and/or fiddlesticks near his or her books.

- Toss a couple of appealing graphic novels and/or magazines into the bathroom.

- Place a few magazines, newspaper articles, or books on the kitchen table where the kids eat their breakfast. Turn off the TV in the breakfast area.

- Make reading more attractive than an alternate activity such as home or yard maintenance. In a calm voice, you can ask your adolescent who is hunched over his or her smartphone like a mother emu protecting her egg, "You have the opportunity to read for a half hour or clean out the fridge for a half hour. It's completely up to you." A variation on this could be, "Would you like to rake up all the damp leaves in the yard, or read for the amount of time that it takes to rake the leaves?"
- Some parents shut down all screens at 8:00 p.m. during the summer. Their kids protest, complain, get bored beyond the point of complaining, and start reading at about 8:30 p.m. When we visit my mom, she gets my son off her desktop computer by shutting down the power to an entire floor of her house.
- Managing cell phone and laptop use at night during the school year is a challenge. This is because adolescents use their phones for practical purposes. They text questions about assignments to classmates. They use the calculators on their phones to do math problems. They create quizlets to study for tests and refer to photos of their teachers' board notes. They work on presentations on Google Docs, where teachers leave notes. On a typical school night, my teens flip between social media and schoolwork, between precalculus problems and videos of the water-bottle flip challenge. The solution that works for us is to have cell phones off by 8:30 p.m. (ideally) and unplug the Wi-Fi to the entire house by 9:30 p.m.

Make the Reading Process Enjoyable

Adolescence is a time of growing autonomy. Kids want to control their own lives. Reading experts advise to let your kid pick what he or she reads and when. As long as he or she gets a half hour of reading for pleasure done, great.

After an adolescent skims the Internet for hours, it can take a while for him or her to adjust to consuming long-form sentences that build into paragraphs and chapters. Some great fiction starts slowly as characters and settings are introduced. Encourage your adolescent to persevere and read at least three chapters of a book before abandoning it. (You could volunteer to read a chapter out loud to get the process started.) If your adolescent actively dislikes a book after reading several chapters, allow him or her to pick a new one.

Once your kid finds a good book, encourage him or her to read for twenty to thirty minutes a day to stay in the flow of the story. They need not be thirty consecutive minutes. This time can be ten minutes before bed, ten minutes while waiting for the bus, ten minutes at the orthodontist office, and ten minutes at a sibling's soccer practice. Leave magazines in the car, and encourage kids to always keep a book in their backpack or on their phone.

Read the first chapter, back cover, or a few pages of your kid's book so you can chat about it. Listen if your son or daughter tells you about an exciting part or reads a sentence from a book. But please do not require book reports or the completion of impromptu vocab quizzes when your kids are reading for pleasure.

Modeling Reading

Experts declare that the enjoyment of books starts at home. We are the commercial for reading. Kids learn from watching the adults in their lives. The more we read in front of them, the more we advertise the importance of reading. You can read silently, out loud, or do both.

How else can parents model reading? Talk about books in front of your kids. Read e-mails, articles, and movie reviews out loud. Give books to each other for birthdays. Listen to audiobooks in the car. Read the newspaper in the morning over coffee. If you are in a book club, mention what you like about it or what you are reading. On a slow weekend or vacation morning, have your partner, or anyone who is staying with you, announce that he or she is grabbing a book and reading on the couch. Have him or her ask the kids to sit down and join in to read for an hour.

Read two or three paragraphs of an interesting article out loud. My adolescents have been intrigued by articles on the following topics: convict escapees, bear attacks, asteroids that may or may not hit Earth, and the giant-python problem in Florida.

People (Besides You) Who Can Encourage Your Kid to Read

Adolescence is a time of growing independence. While we adore our kids and recognize that they are wonderful people who love us deeply, sometimes they don't want our sage parental advice—or our company. But a third party can encourage them to crack open a book. The following is a list of people besides you who can get your kids reading:

- **A reading buddy** can be a classmate, a neighborhood kid, a teammate, or a cousin who is your child's age or slightly older. Your kid has to like spending time with this person. The more your kid admires this person, the better. Take your adolescent and his or her reading buddy to the bookstore or the library to peruse books and magazines. Let them wander through the shelves on their own. Don't follow them. Don't make book suggestions. Do consider buying them coffee, ice cream, or a snack right after visiting the books. Do ask which book looked interesting.

If your adolescent balks at the idea of bringing a friend to the bookstore or library, make it a surprise. While driving your adolescent and reading buddy home from a sports practice or other activity, let them know that you need to pick up a book for yourself. Pull into your local bookstore parking lot and point out it's too cold/hot/boring for them to sit in the car and wait for you. They need to come into the bookstore or library.

- **A "cool" aunt or uncle or family friend** who loves books can encourage your adolescent to read. He or she can share recommendations and pass on books to your kid. Author and uncle Frank Bruni writes, "I'm incessantly asking my nephews and nieces what they're reading and why they're not reading more. I'm reliably hurling novels at them, and also at friends' kids. I may well be responsible for 10 percent of all sales of 'The Fault in Our Stars.'"

- **Grandparents** want to connect with their grandkids and usually have the time and inclination to read. Ask your parents or in-laws to take your kid to the library and pick out a book, or to drive him or her to a bookstore. They can play an audiobook or podcast in the car if they are taking grandkids to activities.

- **Babysitters.** If you're traveling and hire a babysitter to stay with your preteens, she can encourage them to read by sharing her favorite books and chatting about what the kids are reading for school.

- **Teachers.** If your teenage son likes his language-arts teacher, he will listen when the teacher talks about his or her best-loved books. Science teachers often have a classroom library of engaging books that your teen can borrow. My son's wonderful eighth-grade science teacher encourages reading by talking about his book club and sending out daily e-mails with interesting science articles to parents and students. Encourage your kids to ask their teachers for reading recommendations. You can also e-mail his or her teacher for recommendations and the best ways to encourage your kid to read for pleasure.

- **Drama directors or singing coaches.** Acting classes, singing lessons, and participating in school plays require students to read lyrics and scripts. Good actors also read books related to their roles in order to learn about a character's internal motivations, relationships, and living conditions. If your daughter has a role in the musical *Wicked*, her drama teacher can encourage her to read the novel *Wicked: The Life and Times of the Wicked Witch of the West* and *Dorothy and the Wizard of Oz*.

- **Authors.** When Rick Riordan, author of the best-selling Percy Jackson series, appeared in Nashville, he was greeted by cheering fans waving giant inflatable pencils. The audience laughed and clapped throughout his hilarious presentation and book promotion; it was a rally for reading.

- **Volunteer coordinators.** Teens may need community-service hours as part of their high-school graduation requirements. They can read books aloud to senior citizens, individuals who are blind, or hospital patients. Teens can tutor elementary-school-age students and read to them or volunteer to read aloud to preschoolers at the local library.

- **Comic-con organizers.** If your adolescent loves graphic novels, fantasy, and science fiction, and is up for rubbing shoulders with superheroes, wizards, and zombies, take him or her to a comic-con. The main comic-con, which is held annually in San Diego, draws about 130,000 costumed adults each year.

(Wizard World Comic-Con is smaller and tours most major cities in the United States.) At comic-con, adolescents can meet their favorite graphic novelists, science-fiction authors, and fantasy authors like Sarah Maas. (Check the websites to see which authors are scheduled to attend.) The enthusiasm for storytelling that motivates adults to dress like Captain America and Tinkerbelle is contagious.

Talking about Books

Teens often don't want to talk about school, their social life, their job, or their future. Books, like movies, are a neutral, acceptable topic. When you are in the car or eating lunch, ask your teen or preteen about what he or she is reading. Ask what he or she likes or dislikes about the book. Inquire about his or her favorite characters. If you haven't read the book and have no idea what it's about, show that you're listening by paraphrasing what your kid says.

Reading Aloud with Adolescents

In *The Read-Aloud Handbook*, Jim Trelease encourages parents and grandparents to continue to read aloud to their preteens and teens. While most parents (including me) stop reading out loud to our kids when they reach age ten or eleven, no one is ever too old to be read to. After reviewing Trelease's book, I started reading aloud to my sixth grader as she got ready for bed. Interesting nonfiction books with two-page chapters worked well. (We found that good fantasy and mystery novels are a little too exciting right before bed: sleep was delayed by repeated requests for "just three more pages.") Listening to me read a minichapter from *Women in Science: 50 Fearless Pioneers Who Changed the World,* and *Mistakes That Worked: 40 Familiar*

Inventions and How They Came to Be helped my twelve-year-old fall asleep.

Not only does reading aloud get adolescents interested in books and enhance their ability to concentrate, it can also be a way for parents to address social and family issues. When you read a book like *Al Capone Does My Shirts* aloud, you and your kid learn about the protagonist's challenges with his disabled sister. It's fodder for discussion, especially for families with similar situations. Instead of lecturing your seventh grader about social media and friends who are bad influences, you can read aloud *Goodbye Stranger*, by Rebecca Stead, which explores these topics. After you read a chapter or a riveting scene, you could ask your kid how he or she would handle the situation.

Kids know that everyone is busy. Taking the time to read a book aloud sends the message that it's something valuable. Some parents do all the reading, others have their kids read a chapter to them aloud, and some alternate reading aloud with their children. Try to pick a book that everyone will enjoy. (Graphic novels and comics generally don't work well.) Here are some books that do:

- *The Alchemist*, the young adult version of *Unbroken*, and the first books of the Percy Jackson and *Harry Potter* series, which can launch kids on reading the rest of the series
- Roald Dahl and Louis Sachar books
- *Out of My Mind*, by Sharon Draper
- *Ella Enchanted*, by Gail Carson Levine

If your son complains that he is too old to be read to and it's "baby-ish," ask him to read a chapter to you while you get dinner ready. Or he can listen while you read, and if he still dislikes it, he can switch to an audiobook.

Eight

READING REWARDS: SHOULD WE USE THEM? DO THEY WORK?

The most direct way to help your adolescent to become a lifelong reader is through encouragement, modeling, getting the right books in his or her hands, and making sure he or she reads them. Ideally, reading will become habitual; it will just be something your family does every day, like taking care of your pets. Then, there is no need for external reading rewards or punishments associated with reading. The satisfaction and enjoyment of reading a good book is the intrinsic reward. Being swept away by a great story keeps your adolescent reading. Gaining new information about a favorite activity is the reward. Parents don't need to bother with extrinsic prizes. (If you are on this path, congratulations! Skip right ahead to the next chapter, on summer reading.)

But for some emerging and dormant teen readers, it can be a daily struggle to get them to open a book. (And by struggle, I mean arguing, protests, and tears over being "forced to read" against their will.) Reading specialists like Penny Kittle stress that kids should be invited into reading. The invitations should involve "suggestions and encouragement."[1]

But what if your emerging or dormant reader rejects all invitations and books, including those that usually hook? What if you followed the previous suggestions for finding the right book—followed them, in fact, to a T—and your kid still says he hates reading? What if reading for pleasure has become a disagreeable battle of wills between you and your adolescent?

Then step back, take a deep breath, and try a different approach. It's time to consider offering reading rewards.

Reading Incentives, Rewards, and Bribes: Do They Work? Should You Use Them?

Brace yourself. We approach one of the most controversial subjects in the adolescent reading world—whether to use incentives, rewards, and bribes to get kids to read. Many reading experts feel that reading rewards are useless, and worse, detrimental. They point out that kids are not intrinsically motivated to read when you reward them by paying a penny a page or five bucks for a long novel. Adolescents tend to stop reading when you stop using rewards; they think, "Why should I read this book if I'm not getting paid?"

Yet, many parents, according to my unscientific poll of asking friends at a summer barbeque, use rewards for summer reading. They point out that libraries and schools offer summer reading incentives such as ice-cream parties, contests, and drawings for e-readers. But should we use rewards? And what really works?

First, let's address what everyone agrees does not work: reading bribes. Do not waste your breath offering bribes; they simply aren't effective. Bribery, unlike a reward, is given *before* a behavior occurs. (Such as when you hand a lollipop to your toddler before heading into the supermarket, and she still screams for the Oreos in aisle 6.) A reward is something given *after* completion of a task. Rewards, like the dog treats that Fido receives for sitting or lying down, have been successfully altering animal and human behavior for centuries. Teens and preteens are familiar with rewards. Their paycheck for bagging groceries at Kroger is a kind of reward. So is the cash they get for babysitting the neighbor's unruly kids.

Experts advise that if you are going to use rewards, make reading the reward. For example, after your teenage daughter finishes a novel, treat her to a trip to Barnes & Noble to pick out a new book. Allow your eleven-year-old son to stay up past his bedtime to finish a Louis Sachar novel. If your teen is busy reading, allow him or her to skip folding the laundry.

But what if you have a teen who refuses to open a book? A reward of reading additional books is not going to motivate him or her. Reading expert Daniel Willingham, author of *Raising Kids Who Read*, states in an NPR interview, "My recommendation is that a reward not be the first thing you try. But if it is the only way to get a kid to read, then I would certainly consider it."

So, there we have it. If you have a highly resistant reader, it's time to up the ante.

The reward for reading needs to be in your adolescent's current currency. It should be something he or she covets and can earn over a period of time. Your teen can earn the reward by paying part of it with his or her own money and reading three or four books..

For example:

- In May, look for upcoming local concerts in August and September. If your teen daughter is dying to see Katy Perry on September 16, agree that she will need to read four books over the summer and pay for half of the price of the ticket (or however much you think she should contribute). Your adolescent owns picking the books, finding the time to read them, and discussing the books with you. (The books need to be on her current reading level.) We did this with my older daughter for her ten-week summer break. Our goal was to be as uninvolved as possible. We didn't remind her to read. This was her project. If she didn't finish the four books, her father or I would be happy to attend the Katy Perry concert in her place. My daughter loved the books she picked and became an engaged reader for the summer.

- Require that your kids earn—through a combination of reading multiple books and using their own money—things they *really* want. This could include iTunes downloads, staying up late, video games, beauty products, piercings, homemade dinner requests, sports gear, "cool" sneakers, hair highlight kits, cellular minutes, and painting their room a new color.

Where do adolescents get the money to earn the aforementioned rewards? They can babysit, pet-sit, be a mother's helper, or do yard work or chores for neighbors, friends, and relatives. They can offer music lessons or basketball lessons, or tutor neighborhood children. Kids in our town referee soccer, baseball, and basketball games starting at age twelve. They bag groceries or work at the local Sonic when they turn fourteen. At sixteen, they work at ice-cream stores, restaurants, and jumpy places.

Other variations on reading currency:

- Require your child to "buy" his or her screen time: an hour of PlayStation for an hour of reading. Or how about a half hour of reading in order to watch an episode of *The Office*?

- Insist that your kids read the book or listen to the audiobook before they earn watching the movie. As an added incentive, you could take them to the midnight movie premiere or award them an endless supply of Milk Duds and Raisinets.

If you successfully use a reward system to encourage piano or clarinet practice, it may be applicable to encouraging reading. Parents of budding musicians say rewards motivate their adolescents to pick up the violin or tuba. Piano teachers and parents use punch cards, checklists, or "music bucks" to track practice times and to allow kids to earn rewards such as tickets to a local musical, the opportunity to record a song in a studio, or a cool T-shirt depicting a favorite musician. For reading-related rewards, parents can offer tickets to a local play of a book their kid loved, a ticket to an author meet-and-greet, or the graphic novel of Wonder Woman if your kid loved the movie. Or, record them reading their favorite part of a book and mix it into a rap song.

What about making reading a required part of your adolescent's life? Reading is just something he or she does every day, like walking the dog or brushing his or her teeth. Requiring reading can work well. It depends on the personality of your adolescent and his or her reading attitude. Instituting daily half-hour reading time makes reading neither a reward nor a punishment. Required reading at home worked well for my kids during elementary school and sixth grade.

As discussed in the introduction, kids' attitudes toward reading can change as they grow. If reading becomes a battle of wills, it sucks the fun out of it and can lead to fake reading. Fake reading occurs when your teen daughter has a paperback open on the kitchen table as she furiously texts on her smartphone, which is hidden under the table leaf. Or your preteen son states that he is going to his room to finish a book, and you hear the constant thumping of a minibasket-ball dunked into the mini-net attached to his door. The goal is to get your adolescents to want to pick up a novel. If he or she is fake reading or strongly resisting, then you could look into the possibility of using rewards.

Nine

Summer Reading and Traveling with Books, Audiobooks, and Podcasts

Summer is prime reading-for-pleasure time. Unlike the school year, when adolescents are tied up with homework and extracurricular activities, summer offers ten long weeks to enjoy books. Many parents report that their teens develop a love of books over the summer. (I can vouch for this. My daughter becomes an engaged reader in June and July and then goes into semidormancy when school starts in August.)

Educators want students to avoid the dreaded "summer slide," which is the documented decline in reading skills that occurs over months when kids are out of school. The simple remedy to the summer slide—according to a Harvard researcher, Jimmy Kim—is for students to read four or five books over the summer break and talk about what they read. Kim suggests, "Ask questions about the story…summarize or ask the child to summarize, and reread hard-to-understand passages. Essentially, make reading more of an interactive process in order to boost fluency and comprehension."[1]

Five books may be an easy achievement for devoted readers and a daunting number for dormants. If you're lucky, your school mandates that students read four books over the summer and allows students to select at least three of them. Several private schools near us do this.

In May or June, have your adolescent write out a five-book "to be read" list, which includes any school-assigned summer reading. If your kid wants to include graphic novels, that's fine. (Since my son can whip through a graphic novel in three hours, I count them as a quarter equivalent of a YA novel.) Ideally, your kids will have jotted down book suggestions that they heard about during the school year. If they haven't, they can check in with friends and family members for recommendations. Or have them scan the YA bestseller lists, Goodreads.com, popular YA book trailers on YouTube, or the list of books that hook in chapter 6. Another idea is to review a list of upcoming, unreleased movies and TV series that are based on YA books.

You may ask, "But what if my teen is traveling or working as a lifeguard this summer? Or is away at camp? She doesn't have time to read."

Adolescents can read at breakfast; at the pool; at the beach; while waiting for siblings at their activities; or at the doctor's office, dentist, or the hair salon. They can read after lunch when it's too hot for the beach or the pool. They can read or listen to audiobooks in planes, trains, buses, and automobiles. Very busy people make time to read. Bill Gates has a hectic schedule but reveals, "I've been reading about a book a week on average since I was a kid. Even when my schedule is out of control, I carve out a lot of time for reading."[2] If your adolescent has time to text, he or she has time to read.

You can encourage reading in the following ways:

Read along with your adolescent. After your son or daughter has picked a book and has started reading it, get your own copy from the library. My fifteen-year-old and I did this with Jojo Moyes's *Me Before You* and two of Sara Maas's books. We chatted about our favorite parts of the books and which characters we loved or despised. It was thoroughly enjoyable.

Implement a family reading hour. Family members sit around and read in proximity to each other. You don't have to be snuggled together into a "reading boat" or even on the same couch. Just hang out with your books, articles for work, newspapers, or e-readers in the same room or part of the yard.

Hold a family book chat. Pick a night for everyone in the family to chat about whatever he or she is currently reading. (It can be for pleasure, work, or school.) Each person brings reading material to the table and talks about what they like or dislike about their current book. Siblings may want to read the books they hear about. Serve a favorite dessert to go along with the chat. Family book chat was easy to set up—all I did was buy the key-lime pie—and my adolescents enjoyed it.

Enhance interest with activities and movie trailers. After reading Veronica Roth's *Divergent*, where adolescents are sorted into groups according to personality traits, my daughter spent two days giving our family *Divergent* aptitude tests that she found online. This her kept interested in the trilogy, as did viewing short trailers of the movie, which she could see after finishing the book.

Read subtitles and closed captions. Studies show that same-language subtitling (SLS) can improve student comprehension skills. In one study students who read karaoke-type subtitles while listening to Broadway shows like *Cats* were better able to decode words and sentences than the control group that did not use captions.[3]

TVs are equipped with closed captioning—just hit the "CC" button. Encourage your kids to watch a muted show or movie while reading the captions. My husband and son watch football with captions while listening to Rush and other hard-rock bands. While Geddy Lee jams "Tom Sawyer" on his electric guitar, they read the commentator's words as they wrap around the bottom of the screen. Teens, including my niece, love the hit Japanese reality-TV show *Terrace House*, which is subtitled. They watch and read while six attractive strangers live in a house in Tokyo.

Book swap with friends. This was a hit with my younger daughter and her ten- to twelve-year-old friends. A book swap is easy to execute; the version below requires minimum adult effort. A book swap is a great way to encourage preteens to share what books they like and what they are currently reading.

Here is how the book swap worked:

- Invite seven to ten of your kid's friends who like to read to bring books that they enjoyed to your house. Our book swap was for two hours, from 4:00 p.m. to 6:00 p.m. on a Friday afternoon. I supplied the snacks and drinks. My eleven-year-old and her friend decorated the house with leftover birthday party streamers and balloons, which kept them busy and made it festive.
- After the guests arrive, serve the snacks, and put all the books on a table so the kids can check them out. Put large Post-its and pens on the table.
- The girls wrote a short description of the book they brought on the Post-its. They decided to sit in a circle on the living room floor and take turns talking about their book. (This was a group of unusually self-directed girls. I could have gone to the mall for the afternoon, and they could have competently run the whole swap .)
- Write a number, representing each attendee, on a scrap of paper. Fold up the numbers and place them in a bowl. With

eyes tightly shut, each girl picks a number from the bowl. The person who picked number 1 picks the first book. The person with number 2 picks either number 1's book or one of the other books in the center of the circle—and so on. Once a book had been chosen three times, it couldn't be "stolen." There was one popular novel that two girls both badly wanted. This was resolved when the picker promised to pass the coveted book on after reading it.

- After swapping books, the girls acted out their favorite Disney movie scenes for each other. This had absolutely nothing to do with the book swap. They made up this activity on the fly, and it kept them busy until their parents arrived.

Insist that your teen keeps a "to be read" list (TBR). Does your teen keep a list of the latest downloadable iTunes songs? Or a record of the Ulta hair products she hopes to purchase? A TBR is another list for teens to keep on their cell phone, agenda, or calendar. A TBR addresses the complaint that there are "no good books to read" and encourages adolescents to get a reading life. Suggestions from friends, relatives, and classmates can go on the TBR. Encourage your kids to google books which are becoming movies or TV shows, and add them to their TBR.

Research family topics. Ask your teens to research and plan a family vacation by reading online articles from reputable sites. If your adolescent is saving up to buy a used car, have him or her research the safest cars for teens from sites like ConsumerReports.org or USnewsreports.org. Anything that is a big purchase that you help fund (think cell phone, pet, trip, decorating his or her room) can be made into a research project that involves reading.

My preteen's research project was investigating the pros and cons of adding another member to our family. For several months we were concerned that Mickey, our current Chihuahua-terrier-Chow mix, was suffering from "single dog syndrome" (SDS). Mickey craved interaction; he was never happier than when he was wresting a pack of large dogs in the mud at the dog park or jumping on the neighbor's poodle. At home, Mickey's constant need to be petted and compulsive licking of every surface of our uncovered skin made us wonder, "Is Mickey sending us a message?"

My daughter's conclusion, after reading *Modern Dog* magazine articles like "How to Understand Your Dog's Bark and Read Your Dog's Tail" was: "Mickey is trying to tell something. Mickey needs and wants a companion, someone to lick besides us." My daughter did such a good job researching the issues surrounding SDS that we agreed to welcome a second dog into our home. While Cash, Mickey's sixty-pound canine companion, is working on his own issues (counter surfing and body-slamming visitors), Mickey is no longer lonely. Granted, there are challenges having a younger brother three times your size with the personality of *Old School's* Frank the Tank. Mickey on occasion looks at us searchingly, silently asking, "What have you done?" But on most days, he is happily playing chase and hiding rawhide bones from his brother.

Encourage your kids to learn more about a song, play, or music they love. After listening to the *Hamilton* soundtrack for the thousandth time, my youngest and her friends googled "Hamilton," "Burr," and the "Schuyler sisters" to read about how long they lived and what happened in their lives. They read the lyrics of the musical, dressed up, and sang along to the CD. My daughter also consumed Elizabeth Cobb's historical novel *The Hamilton Affair*, which is about Hamilton's relationship with his wife.

If your adolescent enjoys a play, artist, or movie, encourage him or her to read more about that interest.

Summer Online Classes and Websites

Many universities and private entities offer summer online classes for adolescents. Teens may take a class to get ready for the school year, to augment a college application, or to explore a topic of interest.

ONLINE CLASSES

My fourteen-year-old daughter, who likes science, took an eight-week high-school-level chemistry course online from a well-known university. We thought she would be performing exciting experiments in her room. But instead of creating exploding volcanoes and making liquid-nitrogen ice cream, she had weekly quizzes on the periodic table and tests on the mechanics of neurons. While my daughter read textbooks for this online class, she disliked it. In retrospect, we should have reviewed the syllabus carefully and asked about the workload prior to paying for the class.

There are a multitude of structured online summer classes that involve reading. Here are few of them:

- Khan Academy is a free site that offers video and PowerPoint lessons on hundreds of topics. (The videos contain subtitles.) Besides computer-programming classes, teens can check out classes on cosmology and astronomy, and dozens of other topics.
- Check out the Virtual High School (http://vhslearning.org/). For a fee, this nonprofit offers four-week online summer classes like
  - Mission to the International Space Station. This course treats participants as members of a class of cadets, in training for their first mission to space. Cadets undergo preflight training, launch into space, and arrive at the International

Space Station (ISS). Cadets consider the challenges and rewards of working on the ISS, learn to adapt to life in space, and observe Earth from orbit.

o Criminology. Students are immersed in the middle of several crime scenes. They perform psychological autopsies on the victims and pick up clues that will shed light on the personality of the killer.

o Solar Energy Design. Using a computer-aided-design and simulation tool called Energy3D along with Google Earth, students construct a model of their chosen residence, design a solar panel array for it, and evaluate how the design meets the challenge of maximizing electrical output while minimizing cost.

• My thirteen-year-old son had a good experience with online summer reading, and it did not cost a cent. Since he is interested in space exploration, we told him to go to NASA's website and read about one mission a day and tell us about what he learned. NASA's website (nasa.gov) is vast. He stuck to the mission section and focused on the major missions like the Mars Explorer.

• The stories section of the *National Geographic* website (national geographic.com) has fascinating articles and beautiful photos. Popular videos like "Orcas Take Down Whale in Coordinated Attack" are embedded in articles so kids can read about what they watch. Over the summer, I occasionally sent my kids to that site to read three or four articles, pick a favorite, and tell us about it over dinner or breakfast.

• Randall Munroe's What If website (https://what-if.xkcd.com/122/) provides page-long answers to absurd hypothetical questions like "What if I made a lava lamp out of real lava? How close could I stand to watch it?" or "What if the New

Horizons Spacecraft hits my car?" My eleven-year-old enjoyed reading this site as well as Google's Made with Code, where she learned how to design emojis and re-create scenes from the movie *Wonder Woman*.

- Teens may be intrigued by "Solve the Outbreak" on the Centers for Disease Control and Prevention (CDC) website (https://www.cdc.gov/mobile/applications/sto/web-app.html). Once teens pick a viral-outbreak scenario such as "Breathless in the Midwest" or "Birthday Party Gone Bad," they read paragraphs of clues and data charts and answer questions.

Traveling with Books, Audiobooks, and Podcasts

Anticipating a vacation can just be just as fun as the trip itself. Build excitement and read about your destination via articles, guidebooks, and fiction set in the location of your vacation, or check out some regional cookbooks.

Heading to Disney? Preteens can review guidebooks, novels like Ridley Pearson's *Kingdom Keepers* series, and short biographies such as *Who Was Walt Disney?*, by Whitney Stewart. Encourage your teen to read about the rides and make a list about which parks and roller coasters he or she wants to hit.

Traveling to San Antonio? Nathan Hale's *Alamo All-Stars* graphic novel makes the Texas Revolution come to life. Or how about reading Louis Sachar's *Holes*, which is set in Texas? Encourage your adolescent to research and pick a restaurant or activity to try in San Antonio. Read an article at dinner that reviews Six Flags San Antonio's scariest roller coasters or Sea World San Antonio's dolphin show.

Have everyone pack a book, and then throw a few extra paperback books that hook into your suitcase. There is often more downtime during a vacation than we anticipate. If you are going camping, where there is no Internet reception, or to a country that has limited cell service, there will be plenty of opportunities for adolescents to read.

If you can convince your adolescents to leave their smartphones and other screens at home, kudos to you; however, the majority of teens and preteens strongly prefer to keep their phone within a one-foot radius of their thumbs at all times. In order to avoid a screen-focused vacation, consider setting up general times for reading and social media. For example, screens are fine to use in the hotel room at night but are off during the day. Or have tech time after lunch, but not during a morning excursion to the beach. (Be prepared to model these guidelines yourself.)

If you travel outside the country, cellular data can be expensive. Tell your teens that it's just too costly for them to use their phones and they need to keep them in airplane mode. When we stay in a VBRO apartment with spotty Wi-Fi or reach our monthly cellular-data limit, it's a good reason to turn off our screens and pick up a book. If we're in a condo with excellent Wi-Fi, I search for the router and unplug it for the morning.

Finally, there are people who plan a vacation around a teen's or preteen's favorite book. We have friends who traveled to Universal Orlando to experience the Wizarding World of Harry Potter after their kids completed the seven-book series. Another family traveled to Clearwater, Florida, to visit Winter the Dolphin because their daughter loved the book *Dolphin Tales*.

Long Car, Bus, Train, or Plane Rides: Audiobooks and Podcasts

When your adolescent is trapped in a car, plane, train, or bus for a long trip, encourage him or her to read or listen to an audiobook.

(Download audiobooks prior to the trip from the library or a source like Audible or iTunes.) During extended travel, we often encounter cellular dead zones and our phones run out of juice, both of which are opportunities to listen to audiobooks. Heated radio-station debates (should we listen to rap, country, pop, or hard rock?) can be easily resolved by switching to a popular audiobook. Audiobooks with terrific narrators can captivate your entire family. Here are some of the most frequently downloaded audiobooks that adolescents enjoy: *Turtles All the Way Down* and other John Green books, *The Giver*, the *Harry Potter* series, *The Hate U Give*, *Geekerella*, and *The Graveyard Book*.

Podcasts are audio files that can be about any topic—food, sports, money, or favorite TV shows. They sound like talk-radio shows and run for about forty-minute segments. We download ours from iTunes, and they are usually free. Most people listen to podcasts from their mobile phone, often during their commute to work. (But you can listen to a podcast from any computer that is linked to the Internet and has a working speaker.)

There is a podcast for every interest. If your teen loves Taylor Swift, the *Gilmore Girls*, and gourmet food, she may enjoy the following podcasts: *Taylor Talk, Gilmore Guys,* and *Sporkful.* Some podcasts have seven chapters; others have hundreds of segments. For long car trips, download eight to ten that may catch your kid's attention.

The following is a list of podcasts that are popular with preteens and teens.

PODCASTS FOR AGES 10 AND UP

- *Brains On!* Science podcasts for kids. Episodes feature topics like "Exploding Engines," "Why Is the Ocean Salty?," and "Slime—What Is It and Why Are We So Obsessed?"

- *Wow in the World*. This podcast focuses on science, technology, and new discoveries. Hosts explore questions like "Where is the happiest place on earth?" and "What in the world is all that junk floating around in the earth's orbit?"
- *The Unexplainable Disappearance of Mars Patel*. Eleven-year-old Mars Patel investigates the mysterious disappearance of two of his friends.
- *Kid Friday*. A technology show hosted by a dad and his daughters, who discuss the latest apps, computers, websites, and other technology.
- *Stuff You Missed in History Class*. This podcast explores topics that are not found in textbooks, such as the origin of cheese—a food that has been around for nine thousand years—and historical mysteries like who was the real Robin Hood.
- *Short and Curly*. Entertaining British hosts discuss ethics and answer questions like "Who gets saved first in a fire?" and "Can you really trust a robot?"

Podcasts for Ages 14 and Up

- *This American Life*. Each episode focuses on a theme and covers everything from what babysitters really do when the parents leave the house, to break-up songs, to kids that were switched at birth.
- *Serial*. This podcast reinvestigates the 1999 murder of high-school student Hae Min Lee and raises questions about the convicted killer's guilt. This was originally aired in 2014 and was a megahit. (There is strong language in this podcast, so parents may want to listen to it first to determine if it's appropriate for their kid.)

- *Locked Up Abroad.* Based on the hit National Geographic TV show, this podcast explores what it is like in the split second when you realize you are about to be locked up in a foreign country—possibly for life.
- *Welcome to Night Vale.* A creepy and often funny radio show set in the mysterious fictional desert town of Night Vale, where strange things frequently happen.
- *All Songs Considered.* This podcast features new and upcoming musical talents as well as older performers, many of whom are making a comeback.
- *Stuff You Should Know.* From the people behind the website HowStuffWorks, this show explains a variety of topics, from how rabies works to how auto-tune works. There are over one thousand podcasts.
- *Radiolab.* These podcasts explore science and philosophy. Episodes include "Revising the Fault Line: A Fresh Look at How, Why, and Who We Blame" and "Nukes: A Look Up and Down the US Nuclear Chain of Command," a look at who gets to authorize the use of nuclear weapons and who can stand in the way of Armageddon.

Ten

Reading for Pleasure When School Resumes

When the first day of school arrives, many of us look forward to passing the reading baton back to our kids' teachers. We did our best to encourage reading over the summer break. Now it's their turn to keep our kids on the reading track, isn't it?

As mentioned earlier, public-school teachers are pressured to teach to state requirements and don't have much time to encourage reading for pleasure. Language-arts classes are chock-full of worksheets, vocabulary quizzes, and practicing state standards such as "Cite the textual evidence that most strongly supports an analysis of what the text says explicitly as well as inferences drawn from the text."[1]

So how can we help? Here are some ideas:

Reading on the Fly

Adolescents need to keep a book on them at all times during the school day. They can store a book in their backpack, in a big binder, or in a purse, and start thinking of books as being as portable as a smartphone. Opportunities to read on the fly arise throughout the school day, and students need easy access to a book of their choice.

Teachers want kids to read if they finish a test, quiz, or homework early, and students can read during focus or study periods. They can read while waiting to be picked up from school or while waiting for an after-school club or sport to start.

Sustained Silent Reading

Sustained Silent Reading (SSR) and Drop Everything and Read (DEAR) are school reading programs where students self-select books and read them for a set amount of time. Both of these programs have been successfully rolled out across many schools in the United States. There can be a set time when the entire school population (including teachers) reads a book, or SSR can be part of a language-arts class.

Our middle school has school-wide DEAR on Friday mornings, when the entire school, including the teachers, reads for pleasure for forty minutes. (The kids who forget their DEAR books get a "strike"; six strikes equals Saturday detention.) Ask your son or daughter which books his or her classmates are reading; these can go on the "to be read" list.

Required Reading: Select the Most Absorbing Book

In middle school and high school, students often get to choose a book within a genre or from a teacher's list. Unless your adolescent does basic research about the choices, it's just as easy for him or her to pick an enthralling book as it is to select an incredibly boring one. Encourage your teen to read the book reviews on Goodreads and ask siblings and friends for feedback before he or she chooses a book.

When my twelve-year-old had to pick a classic to read for his language-arts class, he selected Charles Dickens's *Great Expectations*—because it was the only classic left on the school library shelf. While struggling with *Great Expectations*, a sprawling novel with a complex narrative and confusing dialects, his enthusiasm for reading plummeted faster than Pip's fortunes. Meanwhile, his friends devoured Jack London's *Call of the Wild*. After taking two weeks to get through the first chapter of *Great Expectations*, my son wisely asked his teacher if he could switch to London's fast-paced *White Fang*, which he found to be "actually a good book." If your kid dislikes a required reading selection, encourage him or her to talk to the teacher. Teachers are usually fine with kids changing books. They want students to read something they like.

Later in the year, my son was required to pick a biography for a school project. This time he asked for input from friends and family and made a great choice: the young adult version of Laura Hildebrand's *Unbroken*. If your kid sees two potential required reading books that look equally interesting, get both books from the library. When searching for *Unbroken*, my son stumbled upon *Samurai Rising: The Epic Life of Minamoto Yoshitsune* and ended up enjoying them both.

My sixteen-year-old daughter randomly chose *Life of Pi* from a list of books supplied by her language-arts teacher and actively disliked it. In retrospect, *The Curious Incident of the Dog in the Night-Time* or *The Alchemist*, which also were also on the list, would have been a much better fit for her. But because she invested time and was four chapters into *Life of Pi*, she stuck with it and grumbled through the rest of the novel. This experience did nothing to enhance her interest in reading. When offered a choice from a list of books or a genre, it's worth your adolescent's time to ask for peer recommendations or quickly peruse online reviews.

Read an Assigned Book Like You Read a Book for Pleasure

When teachers assign a book to be read, annotated, and analyzed chapter by chapter, students lose the flow of the story. In order to stay engaged in the plot, adolescents can read the assigned book like they read a book for pleasure. In other words, skip annotating and consume several chapters at a time. Then, at a later date, go back, reread, and take notes in the chapter that is due.

My son read *Warriors Don't Cry*, which was the assigned class reading in seventh grade, this way and enjoyed it. My sixteen-year-old consumed several chapters of *The Things They Carried* at a time without taking notes. She found this novel about Vietnam soldiers to be completely absorbing when read as a regular book.

Make the Classics Accessible

Many teens ask as they struggle through the classic *Moby-Dick*, "Why do I have to read 822 pages about a crazy guy going whaling and then boiling blubber?" And more generally, "Why do I have to read the classics? What's in it for me?"

The short answer is that the books written or read today have been influenced by the classics. The classics are the touchstone books where great literary themes, ideas, movements, and/or genres started. Reading them helps us better understand our history and books written today. While reading the classics is important, understanding the archaic language, symbolism, and complex themes in these books can be challenging. It can be helpful to point out to your teenage son that he doesn't have to like the story of a classic like *Moby-Dick*, but by reading it and thinking about it, he is going to get something from it. He will be able to understand cultural references to the book and will learn about imagery and the times when it was written.

As a freshman, my daughter was assigned to read Steinbeck's *The Grapes of Wrath*, which she found simultaneously "boring and depressing." She struggled to stay engaged with the novel's pace and language. It helped to remind her that she didn't have to enjoy this classic to get something useful from it. By reading *The Grapes of*

Wrath, she experienced firsthand important events in our country's history: migration, the dust bowl, and the Great Depression.

If your teen or preteen enjoys the fast pace of *The Lightning Thief* or *The Hunger Games,* then the slow, descriptive start of a classic can be daunting. In order to get adolescents over the hump of the first sixty pages, try reading chapters or pages out loud with your teen. Or encourage him or her to listen to the audiobook of the classic. There may also be a good young adult version of the book that has a faster pace.

In order to better understand the classics, adolescents can watch John Green's *Crash Courses* on YouTube. John Green, the author of *The Fault in Our Stars* and other novels, is also known as the "teen whisperer." He explains books like *The Odyssey* in an engaging, relatable way. His first "Crash Course on Literature" explains why we should all read the classics and may help your adolescent appreciate them.

Here are some classics that adolescents may enjoy reading:

- *Call of the Wild,* by Jack London. Teens who are fans of adventure and animal stories may enjoy the tale of a heroic dog who is kidnapped in California and taken to Alaska, where he is trained to be a sled dog.
- *White Fang,* by Jack London. The adventures of White Fang, a wolf-dog, who endures harsh circumstances in the Yukon and at the hands of cruel captors.
- *Pride and Prejudice,* by Jane Austen. For teens who enjoy character-driven romances. Set in England at the turn of the nineteenth century, this is the story of the relationship between the lively Elizabeth Bennett and the rich, handsome, and haughty Fitzwilliam Darcy.

- *Jane Eyre*, by Charlotte Brontë. Jane Eyre is dumped by her cruel aunt into a poor charity school, where she is educated to become a governess. Jane is sent to work at gloomy and mysterious Thornfield Hall and falls for its owner.
- *The Count of Monte Cristo*, by Alexander Dumas. Nineteen-year-old Edmond Dantes is about to marry his longtime love when he is framed for a crime he didn't commit. Dantes is shipped to a dank prison. Once there, he plots an elaborate revenge.
- *The Hound of the Baskervilles*, by Sir Arthur Conan Doyle. The Baskerville family is haunted by a huge, murderous hound. After Sir Charles Baskerville mysteriously dies, Sherlock Holmes and Dr. Watson investigate.
- *The Scarlet Pimpernel*, by Baroness Orczy. During the French Revolution, a mysterious figure known as the Scarlet Pimpernel rescues men, women, and children from the guillotine. While this classic starts slowly, readers will be caught up in the adventure and romance.
- *The Great Gatsby*, by F. Scott Fitzgerald. During the Roaring Twenties, the self-made, fabulously rich Jay Gatsby tries to win back his love, Daisy Buchanan, a beautiful, married socialite.
- *To Kill a Mockingbird*, by Harper Lee. A young girl living in a fictional small Alabama town in the 1930s witnesses her father's representation of a black man accused of raping a white woman and experiences the town's reaction to the trial.
- *And Then There Were None*, by Agatha Christie. Ten strangers are beckoned to an isolated island off the Devon coast. One by one, they are murdered. Once teens get past the first forty pages or so of character descriptions, they will be hooked on this well-plotted mystery.

- *Dracula*, by Bram Stoker. A Victorian vampire novel told mainly through diary entries of the main characters.

Dialect Challenges

When you travel to the south part of Boston, you will hear a different dialect of the English language spoken than if you were relaxing on Bondi Beach in Sydney. Even a simple greeting—"What's doin'?" versus "G'day, mate!"—can be dramatically different. Accents and dialect abound, and at times can cause confusion.

After we moved to the great state of Tennessee, my daughter, who was raised in Pennsylvania, came home from school complaining that her teacher repeatedly called her an "onion," one of her least-favorite vegetables. An onion? Why an onion? my husband and I wondered. She was always such a good student—more like a peach than a pungent bulb that made you cry. Upon further inquiry, we learned that the Tennessee teacher was saying "young'un" (not "onion") as in, "You young'uns will not remember this, but Dollywood used to be just a train ride around the hills and hollers before it got all fancy."

As many of us can attest, regional vernacular exists, and authors employ different dialects to make their characters authentic. Dialects can depict a period of time, where a person lives, or a character's socioeconomic background and education. They can also help the author distinguish between which character is speaking. Authors like Charles Dickens and Emily Brontë effectively use dialects for all these reasons. So did Bram Stoker. The following is from Stoker's *Dracula*, which was first published in 1897: "Ye don't see aught funny! Ha! ha! But that's because ye don't gawm the sorrowin' mother was a hell-cat that hated him because he was acrewk'd—a regular lamiter he was."

While students may be tempted to skip such sentences, what helps is to read dialogue *s-l-o-w-l-y* and out loud. Listening to the audiobook and rereading sections of dialogue may make the language easier to grasp. Understanding another character's reaction or response can reveal the gist of what is said. The more dialect you read, the easier it becomes to comprehend. Our eyes and ears get used to it.

Understanding Historical Customs and Culture

The authors of classics wrote their novels for their contemporaries—not for generation Z living in the twenty-first century. Teens can better understand the classics if they are aware of the historical context in which the books were written. For example, Homer assumes that his readers are familiar with the customs of ancient Greece. If a reader is not, he or she misses out on the poet's themes, allusions, and characterizations. In Homer's *Odyssey*, offering hospitality to anyone who shows up at your doorstep is a mark of good character. But welcoming a stranger into your home would be a sign of stupidity to today's adolescents, who have been raised with ADT alarm systems and "Stranger Danger" classes. By understanding the customs of ancient Greece, students are better able to assess *The Odyssey*'s characters.

When Jane Austen wrote *Pride and Prejudice* in 1796, she expected that her audience understood the social mores of England's landed gentry. If a twenty-first-century adolescent does not, he or she will miss major plot developments. Today's teens read about Lydia running away for the weekend with Wickham and shrug. They wonder, "So Lydia's hooking up with her cute boyfriend. What's the big deal?"

When adolescents understand the historical context of *Pride and Prejudice*, they recognize that Lydia's fling is a disaster. Her selfish rendezvous could destroy her family's reputation and ruin her four sisters' marriage prospects. If they can't marry, they'll be destitute. Unlike today, young women in Austen's novels are dependent on their husbands for their economic status. Who they marry directly affects whether their basic needs of food and shelter will be met. And in order to find an acceptable husband, a woman must possess a "sterling" reputation, which meant no sex or hint of sex before marriage.

Understanding Shakespeare

Language has evolved in the four hundred years since Shakespeare wrote his plays. While Shakespeare contributed close to two thousand words to the English language, it can be hard to understand his verses and puns.[2] Who has sat through *King Lear* or *Richard III*—trying to keep the "thees" and "thines" strait—and not thought, at one point, "What in the world are all these actors talking about?"

Shakespeare's plays were meant to be seen. It's easier to understand the plots and the characters by watching the actors. Shakespeare often employs the art of disguise, faked deaths, and other deceptions. In order to keep track of who is alive and cross-dressing and who is not, try viewing the videos of Shakespeare's plays on YouTube.

The movie versions can make the plays even more accessible. While reading *Romeo and Juliet* as a freshman, my daughter saw the movie version of the play with a young Leonardo DiCaprio. She liked the movie (and Leo). Once she understood the plot, it was easier to focus on decoding the language. Author John Green also offers *Crash Course* videos about Shakespeare's works. He explains *Romeo and Juliet*, *Hamlet*, and Shakespeare's sonnets in segments that are informing and entertaining. Some teachers recommend that their students review SparkNotes' No Fear Shakespeare as a study guide while reading the plays.

The following are movie versions of Shakespeare's plays that teens may enjoy and received good reviews. (Before recommending one to your kid, check the ratings. A few, like *Macbeth* and *Othello,* depict graphic violence.)

- *Romeo and Juliet* (1996), with Leonardo DiCaprio and Claire Danes.
- *Macbeth* (2015), starring Marion Cotillard.
- *Much Ado about Nothing* (1993), starring Kenneth Branagh and Denzel Washington.
- *Hamlet* (1996), with Kenneth Branagh and Billy Crystal.
- *A Midsummer Night's Dream* (1999), with Calista Flockhart.
- *Othello* (1995), with Laurence Fishburne.
- *Julius Caesar* (1953), starring Marlon Brando.
- *Taming of the Shrew* was the basis for the adaptation *10 Things I Hate about You* (1999).

Eleven

Book Clubs Encourage Reading—but Will Your Adolescent Join One?

Recent research shows that the more time teens spend doing in-person activities like sports, hanging out with friends, or club meetings, the happier they are. (The opposite is also true: the more time teens spend on social media, the more symptoms of depression they display.[1]) Rather than lying alone in a dark bedroom viewing Snapchats of sleepovers they weren't invited to, adolescents can boost their moods by joining a book club and connecting with a community of readers.

Many adults love being in a book club. They feel like Gretchen Rubin, the author of *The Happiness Project*, who states, "They [book clubs] are the joy of my life."[2] As the founder of two book clubs (one for tweens and one for adults) and a member of several others, I agree that book clubs can be fun. Reading experts believe that a reading community, whether it's a classroom setting, family members sitting around a table, or an official book club, helps kids develop into lifelong readers.

Parents, if you've lived through book-club drama or if your book club has disbanded due to infighting, you have my sympathy. Keep in mind that the majority of book club experiences are positive. Encourage your child to get involved with one.

Below are three types of book clubs that can work well for adolescents.

Family Book Club

The first is a family "book club." My older daughter and son had no interest in forming an official book club with friends. But they liked it when my husband or I read a book that they selected. We had several successful, unofficial mother-son, mother-daughter, sister-brother book clubs with books like *Unbroken*, which has a young adult version; *The Hunger Games*; and *A Dog's Purpose*. Talking about a book that you both read is a great way to connect. Rather than asking your adolescent about school and receiving a monosyllabic answer, you can discuss Louis Zamperini's imprisonment in *Unbroken* or analyze the love triangle in *The Hunger Games*.

Book Clubs for Ages Nine to Twelve

The second book club that works well is for kids ages nine to twelve. My older daughter and I started one, and it was successful because the focus was on fun. The monthly meetings were like playdates, with good snacks and twenty minutes of book discussion.

Here is how it works:

- Ask friends in the same grade who like to read to join. Each girl had at least one other friend in our book club. At monthly meetings, we had five to nine participants.
- The book club meets once a month at someone's home after school for an hour and a half. The host picks the book,

supplies the snack, and provides an easy craft. (For our craft, the girls drew a picture of a favorite character from the book.)

- A parent organizer sends out e-mails or texts about book selection and meeting time and place.
- Everyone is encouraged to finish the book before the meeting.
- The girls take the bus home together after school, have their snack, talk about the book for about twenty minutes, and then do the craft.
- Once the kids arrive, phones and screens are off and in backpacks.
- They sit in a circle during the discussions. The parent facilitator moves the discussion along by asking the "general book-discussion questions" below.
- Suggested Reading for book clubs ages nine to twelve: *Diary of a Wimpy Kid*, by Jeff Kinney; *Smile* or *Sisters* (graphic novels), by Raina Telgemeier; *Rules*, by Cynthia Lord; *The Tail of Emily Windsnap*, by Liz Kessler. *Out of My Mind*, by Sharon Draper; *Wonder*, by R. J. Palacio; and *Esperanza Rising*, by Pam Munoz Ryan.

General Book Discussion Questions for Almost Any Book

- Who was your favorite character, and why?
- Who is your least-favorite character, and why? How did your least-favorite character's backstory or personal history influence his or her actions?
- How did the characters change or grow during the course of the book?

- What part of the book did you like the most? Was there a scene that you found particularly exciting or emotional?
- What do you think the title of the book means? Would you change it?
- Did you learn something new from reading this book? Did it change your view of a topic or a person?
- What did you think of the structure of the book? (Is the story told from one person's point of view or different points of view? Do certain chapters go back in time?)
- Recap the ending. What did you think of the ending? Did it surprise you? If you didn't like it, how would you change it?
- If there was a sequel to the book, what would you like it to be about?
- If this book was made into a film, which actors should play the main characters?
- If this book has already been made into a movie that you have seen, how are the movie and book different? What did you think of the movie version?
- Have you read any other books by this author? If so, how do they compare?

Book Clubs for Boys Ages Nine to Twelve

Boys' book clubs can be run just like the club described above, but consider having fewer members—between four and seven. Replace the craft with active games like shooting baskets, whiffle ball, or kickball.

Reading suggestions for a boys' book club are the *Diary of a Wimpy Kid* series, by Jeff Kinney; *Big Nate*, by Lincoln Peirce; *Holes*, by Louis Sacher; *Wonder*, by R. J. Palacio; *Crossover*, by Kwame Alexander; and *Al Capone Does My Shirts*, by Gennifer Choldenko.

Teen Book Clubs for Ages Thirteen and Up

Schools and libraries offer teen book clubs. If these groups don't appeal to your adolescent, he or she could start his or her own. A book club can be as casual as three friends reading the same Sarah Dressen teen romance over the summer, or it can be a more-structured, coed book club that meets once a month at Starbucks and only reads science fiction.

However structured, teen book clubs should be run by the adolescent members. The teens—not their parents—decide on what to read and when and where to meet. Parents can suggest guidelines, venues, and food, but the direction of the club has to be driven by the members. Often teen clubs are as much about socializing as discussing the book, and that's OK.

Teens know which of their friends are into reading and might be interested in joining a book club. Anyone who posts what they are reading on Instagram, mentions a book at lunch, or talks about the novels they love during language-arts class could be a potential member.

The following guidelines can help an adolescent book club run smoothly:

- Book clubs need an official or unofficial teen leader to communicate when and where the club is meeting.
- Teens should avoid suggesting their favorite book as a book club selection. (Another member may hate it and point out its flaws.)
- Members can take turns selecting books, or let the leader pick.
- The person who suggested the book can lead the discussion. There may be discussion questions at the back of the book or on the Internet.
- Members who haven't finished the book should come to book club anyway. They may have interesting points of view and add to the discussion.

- Disagreements over books make for interesting conversations. If the discussion gets too heated, the leader can say that it's time to move on and ask the next question.
- If certain members dominate the discussion, try a "let's hear from someone else."
- Smartphones are off unless someone is googling something related to the book and sharing the results with the group.
- Meetings run about an hour and a half. Decide what format works for your group. Adolescents can meet at a coffee shop, Chick-fil-A, a park, or in each other's homes. What works well for my adult book club, which meets monthly in local restaurants, is to request to sit at a round table if available. We catch up on our lives first, and then discuss the book once the food is served.
- How to select books: Members can take turns picking books and leading discussion, or the book-club leader can take suggestions and then pick the books. Teens are busy, so the book should be high interest and a fairly fast read.

    Some good book-club book suggestions are *Eleanor and Park*, by Rainbow Rowell; John Green's *Looking for Alaska*; Sherman Alexie's *The Absolutely True Diary of a Part-Time Indian*; *A Long Walk to Water*, by Linda Soo Park; Nicola Yoon's *The Sun is Also a Star*; and *Divergent*, by Veronica Roth.

Supporting Devoted or Gifted Readers through Book Clubs and Online Groups

Devoted readers maintain double reading lives—one for schoolwork and one for pleasure. As mentioned previously, devoted readers often read above their grade level and enjoy complex novels. These skilled readers whip through books fast. Since teachers tend to focus on students who read below grade level, gifted readers are left to their own devices to find engaging reading material. Teachers may encourage them to bring in their own books to peruse while the rest of the class is completing an assignment.

If you have a fifth grader who is reading at a tenth-grade level, it's challenging to find novels that are appropriate for his or her age and reading level. You don't want your ten-year-old reading *Game of Thrones* or other novels that portray graphic violence or mature topics. Have your gifted reader check out nonfiction such as biographies, or science books like Neil Degrasse Tyson's *Astrophysics for People in a Hurry*. The Young Adult Library Services Association (YALSA) website has a list of award-winning nonfiction books for teens.

Mensa, the high-IQ society, offers a Mensa for Kids Excellence in Reading Program (http://www.mensaforkids.org/achieve/excellence-in-reading/.). This free program lists challenging books by grade level. Many of these books are classics. If your kid finishes reading and rating these books, Mensa will send a Mensa Excellence in Reading T-shirt to him or her. Also, check out Newbery Medal–winning books. You can find a list of them online at the American Library Association website (ala.org.)

Besides participating in online book clubs like Goodreads, gifted readers may want to explore book clubs at the local library and at school. Our middle-school book club participates in an annual Battle of the Books. The Battle of the Books is a quiz bowl where students read books from a list and then compete against another local middle school. Student teams earn points for answering questions about the books on the list. (For more information see, http://www.battleofthebooks.org/what/.)

One of our local middle schools encourages devoted readers to work in the school library, where they have access to new YA releases and recommend books to their peers. If this sounds like something your adolescent may enjoy, contact the school librarian; he or she may welcome student helpers.

Twelve

READING REAL AND FAKE NEWS: WHY YOU SHOULD
CARE WHETHER YOUR KID CAN TELL THE DIFFERENCE

Adolescents read a tremendous amount of news on their phones, and much of it comes from YouTube, Snapchat, and TMZ. The news that they consume is often about their favorite celebrity, athlete, or a catastrophic natural disaster. While adolescents may be up to date on Steph Curry's new $200 million contract and Kylie Jenner's latest lip-fix kit, they may not be reading about politics and historical events that are currently unfolding around them.

Kelly Gallagher writes in *Readicide* that two of the seniors in his class—who were old enough to vote in an upcoming presidential election—thought Al Qaeda was a person named Al. And in two different class periods, he "did not have a single ninth grade student who could identify the vice president of the United States." In order to become informed voters and influencers, we all need to be aware of current events. News can motivate us to become involved with an organization or a cause or to better understand what a classmate's family living overseas may be going through.

In order to educate his students about current events, Gallagher ordered classroom copies of *Newsweek* and had his students read and answer questions about an article of the week. Parents can easily replicate this at home. *Newsweek* or *Time* can be ordered online. Once the news magazine shows up at your home, chat about the articles.

Here are some additional suggestions for encouraging teens to be aware of current events:

- Subscribe to a newspaper or get copies of a relative's or friend's newspaper once that person has finished reading them.
- While you're driving your adolescent, ask him or her to access a reputable news site and tell you about what is happening in the world. If you listen to the news on the radio in the car, talk about it.
- Encourage your teen to write a comment on an article he or she found intriguing or send an e-mail to the reporter to ask a question.
- Adolescents can write about current events for a school newspaper or local-community website. They can be journalists by documenting events such as videotaping a rally or a speech, or writing about them in a blog.

The Problem of Fake News

Besides exposing kids to legitimate news sources, it's worth taking the time to discuss why fake news is detrimental. Deceptive news can affect the outcome of presidential elections, unfairly influencing voters and undermining the democratic process. It can even stir up violence. Fake news is written by people who get paid to lie and manipulate the truth. When we forward misinformation on to friends and family, we're helping these scammers.

Adolescents need to realize that just because they read news on a friend's Snapchat or Facebook page, it doesn't mean it's true. In our digital age, anyone can make up a news story and widely distribute it. There are hundreds of hoax-news websites on the Internet, and many of them are focused on politics. The nonprofit organization FactCheck.org has a list of websites that publish fake stories.

Bogus news can be manufactured as a prank. During a much-anticipated and relaxing family vacation in Florida, my fifteen-year-old, who dislikes germs and avoids anyone with a cold, received a video newscast declaring an Ebola outbreak in our hometown. Frightened, she immediately shared the news with her siblings, and a collective freak-out ensued. After checking several reputable online sources, which did not mention anything about Ebola in Tennessee, my daughter recognized that she had received fake news. She then warned her friends about the video.

There are also satirical news organizations like the *Onion*, which publish articles in jest, such as "Johnson & Johnson Introduces 'Nothing But Tears' Shampoo to Toughen Up Newborns." Some of these articles may appear so real that foreign-media outlets take them as straight news. When the *Onion* reported that lawmakers were threatening to abandon Washington, DC, unless they got a new state-of-the-art capitol with a "retractable rotunda," the *Beijing Evening News* published it as real news.

So how do we figure out what's legitimate news and what's bogus? Fake news gets more sophisticated every day, so we need to critically think about the sources. The International Federation of Library Associations[1] and Facebook post tips on spotting fake news. Here is a summary of their advice:

Tips for Spotting Fake News

Check the author and sources. Who wrote this article? Is he or she a real person? Is the author trying to sell you something? Does he or she have a political agenda? Do a quick Google search to learn more about the source. Also, if the writer doesn't name the experts he or she quotes, you may be reading a fake story.

Hyped-up headlines. Headlines in all caps with exclamation points are often signs of a fake news story. Words like "AMAZING!" "Unbelievable," or "Incredible!" in the headline are clues that you may be reading a fictional story.

Heavily photoshopped pictures. Teens are familiar with Photoshop, an app that can be used to doctor photos before posting them. Be skeptical of any source that is manipulating pictures. In addition, if there are unrelated photos in the story (like people in small bathing suits), it may not be a real story.

Misspellings and triple spaces in the article. If there are a multitude of misspellings, grammatical errors, and gaps between words, you may be reading a false article.

Check the date. Old news stories can be reposted as current.

Excessive ads and pop-ups. Advertisements and jiggling pop-ups asking for your e-mail address or for money or touting a deal that seems too good to be true, could all be signs of a fake news article.

Is it satire? If the story seems outrageous (and hilarious), check the source. It may be a joke. The *Onion* and the *Daily Currant* are two sites of news parody.

Are other reputable media sources reporting the story? Check three other major news sources. If they don't mention anything about the news story you are reading, it could be fictitious.

When you or your adolescent suspect that you received fake news, don't forward it to your friends and family. If you see a bogus story on

Facebook, you can help by reporting it. What if your daughter posts news that she later discovers is false? Encourage her to take down the post and share the real facts.

Thirteen

Frequently Asked Questions Once Your Kid Is on the Road to Reading

After your adolescent reads a book that hooks and is reading for pleasure, questions may arise on what to read next and reading styles. This chapter addresses both of these topics.

My eleven- and fifteen-year-old daughters want to read books with diverse, relatable characters. Can you suggest some good ones?
More of today's authors are writing about characters of different races with a variety of backgrounds and family structures. The nonprofit We Need Diverse Books (weneediversebooks.com) actively promotes diversity in the publishing industry.

Here are some reads your kids may enjoy:

- *Counting by 7s*, by Holly Goldberg Sloan. Willow is a genius who never quite fits in anywhere. After her adoptive parents die in a car crash, she finds a surrogate, diverse family.
- *Flygirl*, by Sherri L. Smith. A girl who loves to fly planes uses her light skin to pass as a white girl in order to join the Women Airforce Service Pilots during World War II.

- *Small Steps*, by Louis Sacher. Two years after being released from a juvenile-correction center, Armpit is home in Texas and trying to straighten his life out.
- *Esperanza Rising*, by Pam Munoz Ryan. A tragedy forces Esperanza to flee to California during the Great Depression and settle in a camp for Mexican farmworkers.
- *Inside Out and Back Again*, by Thanhha Lai. Hà and her family flee their home in Vietnam and immigrate to Alabama. The book is inspired by the author's real life.
- *Ghost*, by Jason Reynolds. "Ghost" Cranshaw has been running ever since the night his father shot a gun at him and his mother. Ghost can join an elite track team, as long as he stops getting into fights at school.
- *Brown Girl Dreaming*, by Jacqueline Woodson. Poems about growing up as an African American in the 1960s and 1970s, living with the remnants of Jim Crow laws.

FOR AGES FOURTEEN AND UP

- *Everything, Everything*, by Nicola Yoon. Because of extreme allergies, Maddie has not left her house for seventeen years, until a handsome boy moves in next door.
- *The Sun Is Not a Star*, by Nicola Yoon. When Natasha, who is twelve hours away from being deported to Jamaica, and Daniel keep running into each other in New York City, could it be fate pushing them together?
- *The Hate U Give*, by Angie Thomas. Starr Carter is with her friend when he is shot and killed. She is the only eyewitness and must decide how much to reveal about what she saw.
- *When Dimple Met Rashi*, by Sandhya Menon. A romantic comedy centered around Indian-American teens whose parents conspire to arrange their marriage.

- *Dear Martin,* by Nic Stone. Seventeen-year-old Justyce McAllister, a scholar-athlete, is roughed up by the police and wonders if he will ever stop being judged by the color of his skin.
- *The Absolutely True Diary of a Part-Time Indian,* by Sherman Alexie. Junior leaves his school on the Spokane Indian reservation to attend an all-white high school.

My son loves Rick Riordan's novels. As of today (May 28) he has read every single one of them. Unfortunately, he refuses to read anything until the next Riordan book comes out at the end of August. How do I convince my son to read something else in the meantime?

It's terrific that your son loves Rick Riordan! Explain to your son that he needs to keep reading for all the brain- and empathy-building reasons discussed in the first chapter of this book. And point out that Rick himself wants your son to read over the summer. Direct your son to the "Rick's Reading Recommendations" page on Rickriordan. com. Once there, he will find a list of books that Rick and his kids, whom he describes as reluctant readers, have enjoyed reading. Here are some of them:

- Suzanne Collins's novels like the *Underland Chronicles* and the Hunger Games series
- *The Alchemyst: The Secrets of the Immortal Nicholas Flamel,* by Michael Scott
- The Leviathan trilogy, by Scott Westerfeld
- Greek mythology anthologies such as *Heroes, Gods and Monsters of the Greek Myths,* by Bernard Evslin
- *Airborn* and *Skybreaker,* by Kenneth Oppel
- The *Alex Rider* series, by Anthony Horowitz
- The *Harry Potter* series, by J. K. Rowling

Any suggestions for what to read after Harry Potter?
The Harry Potter books are one of the best ways to hook preteens on reading.

The series is so absorbing that people who spend months—sometimes years—reading J. K. Rowling's magical stories report experiencing post–Harry Potter depression (PHPD). After finishing the seventh and final book, I remember feeling at a loss and thinking, "What am I going to do with my life now?" No other story seemed remotely as absorbing as the adventures of Harry, Hermione, and Ron. (I desperately missed Hagrid.)

Besides watching the Harry Potter movies, exploring Pottermore.com (J. K. Rowling's official website), and rereading the series, fans can start a new fantasy series. Try these Harry Potter read-alikes:

- The Percy Jackson series, by Rick Riordan
- The Inkheart series, by Cornelia Funke
- *The False Prince*, by Jennifer Nielsen
- The *Fablehaven* series, by Brandon Mull
- *The Golden Compass: His Dark Materials,* by Philip Pullman
- The *Artemis Fowl* series, by Eoin Colfer
- The *Lord of the Rings* trilogy, by J. R. Tolkien
- The *Ranger's Apprentice* series, by John Flanigan
- The Hunger Games series, by Suzanne Collins

My kid loved the Hunger Games trilogy. Can you suggest similar books?
The Hunger Games enthralls thousands of readers. After reading the trilogy and watching the movies, your adolescent may enter a dystopian phase where he or she only consumes novels about teens struggling to survive in harsh, oppressive societies. Both of my daughters went through a long dystopian stage. Rather than analyze why my children wanted to exclusively read dark, gritty novels where the

adult characters are incompetent, corrupt, or dead, I tried to just be happy that they were reading.

Here are some exciting dystopian novels:

- The Maze Runner trilogy, by James Dashner. Thomas wakes up surrounded by strange boys in a world hidden by a terrifying maze.
- The Divergent trilogy, by Veronica Roth. In a world where people are divided into factions based on human virtues, Tris Prior is warned she will never fit into any of the groups.
- *The 5th Wave*, by Rick Yancy. After a series of alien attacks destroy the planet, a teenager searches for her brother and forms an alliance with a mysterious young man.
- The Legend trilogy, by Marie Lu. In this series set in a futuristic Los Angeles, June searches for a renowned criminal in order to avenge her brother's death.
- *Matched*, by Ally Condie. In Cassia's world, the government controls everything and "matches" people to their mates.
- *Gone*, by Michael Grant. After everyone over the age of fifteen disappears from a small California hometown, the teenagers left behind grow strange mutant powers.
- *Ready Player One*, by Earnest Cline. Set in 2044, where reality is an ugly place and people spend all their time plugged into Oasis, a virtual utopian world, trying to figure out clues left by its creator. Whoever finds all three clues inherits incredible wealth.
- *Cinder*, by Marissa Meyer. Cinder, a cyborg hated by her stepmother, becomes involved with a handsome prince.
- *The Red Queen*, by Victoria Aveyard. Mare, a poor commoner with Red blood, is thrown into the Silver-blood court and discovers she has hidden powers of her own.

I don't know if my eleven-year-old daughter is ready to read the graphic violence in *The Hunger Games*. Any advice?

If you're unsure if a book is appropriate for your child, find out more information about the story. You can do this in the following ways:

- Go to Common Sense Media (commonsensemedia.org). This independent nonprofit reviews popular books, movies, and TV shows and assigns a rating of one to five stars for categories like violence, sex, language, positive role models, and drinking and drugs.
- Check out the customer reviews on Amazon and Goodreads to learn more about the story. Read the Amazon editorial review section, which is right above the reader review section. Publications like the *School Library Journal* will describe the ages and/or grades for which the book is recommended.
- Read the book yourself.
- Talk to other parents whose kids have read the book. Ask friends who have read the book if they think it's appropriate for your daughter.

My middle-school daughter wants to read *Gone with the Wind*, which is her best friend's favorite book. I'm appalled by the racism and racist language in *Gone with the Wind*. Should I let her read it?

While *Gone with the Wind* has compelling characters, romance, and an exciting storyline, it's undeniable that the book uses racist language and portrays a romanticized version of slavery and the Old South. But let your daughter read it. If you try to censor it, her friend will slip her a copy, and she will consume it anyway. Nothing intrigues an adolescent more than a banned book or movie. Talk to your daughter about the context in which *Gone with the Wind* was written. You could also encourage her to read a book like Sharon Draper's *Copper Son* or Dean Walter Meyer's *The Glory Field*, which depict lives of American slaves and the real horror of human bondage.

Many of the popular young adult books focus on death, abandonment, and abuse. I'm worried these topics may depress my kid. Can you recommend some lighter books?
We all need a break from heavy reading. Here are some humorous or uplifting books:

For Ages 10 and Up:

- The *Diary of a Wimpy Kid* series, by Jeff Kinney. The humorous adventures of Greg Heffley are depicted in graphic novels.
- *Demon Dentist*, by David Walliams. A poor boy named Alfie has to fend not only for himself, but for an inept parent.
- Calvin and Hobbes books and Gary Larson's *The Far Side* cartoon collections.
- *What If?: Scientific Answers to Absurd Hypothetical Questions*, by Randell Munroe. This book provides scientific answers to absurd questions like "How fast can you hit a speed bump while driving and live?"
- *The Princess Diaries*, by Meg Cabot. A fourteen-year-old living in a New York City loft discovers that she is sole heir to the kingdom of Genoa.
- *The Worst Class Trip Ever*, by Dave Barry. An eighth-grade class trip to the nation's capital quickly escalates into an international incident.
- *Skulduggery Pleasant*, by Derek Landy. Skulduggery Pleasant, a wisecracking skeleton-detective, solves crimes.

- *I Funny*, by James Patterson. Jamie Grimm, a middle schooler who uses a wheelchair, hopes to make it big as the world's first sit-down comic.

AGE 14 AND UP

- *In a Sunburned Country*, by Bill Bryson. This book describes the author's adventures traveling around Australia. *A Walk in the Woods*, where Bryson hikes the Appalachian Trail, may also appeal to adolescents.
- *Is Everyone Hanging out Without Me?* and *Why Not Me?*, by Mindy Kaling. Humorous essays on the author's childhood, college life, and experiences in Hollywood.
- *The Blind Side*, by Michael Lewis. The true story of a family that takes in a homeless teen who goes on to be an NFL player.
- *A Long Way Home*, by Saroo Brierly. A true story of a five-year-old Indian boy who loses track of his family when he falls asleep on a train.
- *Fangirl*, by Rainbow Rowell. Cath, a quirky megafan of a Harry Potter–like series, enters her freshman year at the University of Nebraska and navigates the first year of college, including a romance with a friend.
- *The Hitchhiker's Guide to the Galaxy*, by Douglas Adams. In this humorous science-fiction novel, Arthur Dent travels the galaxy getting into horrible messes and generally wreaking havoc. If your kid enjoys Douglas Adams, have him or her try Terry Pratchett's Discworld series too.
- Books, articles, or columns by David Sedaris or Dave Barry.

My preteen enjoys *Good Night Stories for Rebel Girls,* which we read aloud before she goes to sleep. Can you suggest some similar books?

My eleven-year-old also likes to read about the successful women described in *Good Night Stories for Rebel Girls*. The following are inspiring nonfiction books that your daughter may enjoy:

- *Strong Is the New Pretty: A Celebration of Girls Being Themselves,* by Kate Parker. A photographic collection of girls living and talking about their lives.
- *Bad Girls Throughout History:100 Remarkable Women Who Changed the World,* by Amy Shen. Short stories and water-color illustrations of women who challenged the status quo and changed the rules for all who followed.
- *Women in Sports: 50 Fearless Athletes Who Played to Win,* by Rachel Ignotofsky. Fifty illustrated profiles of talented female athletes.
- *The Gutsy Girl: Escapades for Your Life of Epic Adventure,* by Caroline Paul. A personal memoir of the author's adventures and brief bios of other daring women.
- *Girls Think of Everything: Stories of Ingenious Inventions by Women,* by Catherine Thimmesh. How inventive women turned their ideas into realities.

My daughter downloads her books onto her e-reader from a Kindle unlimited account. She doesn't need to visit our public library for access to books. I spent a lot of time in libraries while growing up, and I'm wondering if I should encourage her to visit one?

In addition to access to books, e-books, audiobooks, and other resources, public libraries offer teen clubs and activities. Encourage your adolescent to visit your local library. Your library may host YA author visits, art- and video-making classes, homework-help centers, creative-writing workshops, movie nights based on best-selling books, Harry Potter Alliance clubs, and many other activities. Some libraries have read-ins, which can include scavenger hunts, author Skypes, book giveaways, pizza, and a sleepover in the teen section.

Is your teen looking for a volunteer opportunity? Libraries offer plenty. Teens and preteens can reshelve books or read to younger kids. Libraries also provide teen-leadership roles through their youth advisory boards. Teens can influence the direction of programming while meeting a new group of friends.

Librarians are a terrific resource. They help adolescents with everything from finding research material for a school project to encouraging them to try a new genre of books. Some librarians assist with ACT and SAT test preparation and even help students with college applications and filling out financial-aid forms.

My son reads the last page of a book first, which drives me crazy. It spoils the excitement of the story. Should I insist that he read the pages in the order the author intended, from the beginning to the end?

As long as your kid eventually reads the entire book, let him read it any which way he wants. (If he is only reading the last twenty-five pages and then casting the book aside, then intervene.) But if he wants to read the ending first, and then read the rest of the book, fine. For mysteries, thrillers, and horror books, knowing the ending and who lives and who dies may make the intensity of the story more manageable.

My preteen daughter usually has two or three novels that she is actively reading. Shouldn't she focus on finishing one book at a time so she keeps track of the plot and characters?

Devoted readers often consume two novels at a time. Many adults listen to an audiobook during their commute to work and read a different book before bed. I read nonfiction early in the morning and murder mysteries at night. Comprehending two different genres of books at two different times of day is easy to manage. It's like watching Ina Garten on the Food Network in the morning and the crime series *Blue Bloods* later in the day. You have no trouble following each show.

What's not so easy is reading two Brandon Sanderson fantasy books and two Tolkien fantasy books at the same time. Long, intricate stories with multiple lands, plots, and dozens of characters can be hard to keep straight. But it is possible. People jot down character lists to refer to while they read. Some adolescents switch between multiple stories, only reading a chapter time. What usually happens is that one book grabs our attention, and we get swept up in the story and end up finishing it first. But if your daughter wants to read several books at a time, let her.

Fourteen

How to Get Your Schools to Promote a Reading Culture

In order to get your kid's school to encourage reading for pleasure, e-mail your child's language-arts teachers and principals and ask for sustained silent reading (SSR) time (SSR may also be called "independent reading" or "DEAR"). You could include links to the article "Sustained Silent Reading Helps Develop Independent Readers (and Writers)" published in *Education World* (updated October 15, 2007). Donalyn Miller's books or her article "Cultivating Wild Readers" on Scholastic.com also explain the benefits of reading in the classroom. Schools can form a student SSR advisory committee to help identify materials and practices that encourage reading for pleasure.

Ask teachers if their students could share book recommendations before summer or winter breaks. While instructors guard their teaching time, peer book recommendations can be made quickly. Each student and the teacher can state one or two sentences about his or her current favorite book. The teacher can post the list of recommended books online in his or her Google classroom so students can access the list when they visit the library.

If your child's language-arts teacher needs books for his or her library or a literacy project, help set up a request on a crowdsourcing site like DonorsChoose.org, where thousands of teachers receive funding for their classrooms. DonorsChoose.org is for "front-line educators," such as teachers, librarians, and guidance counselors, who work with students and teach full time. (They don't accept requests from principals, student teachers, part-time teachers, or PTA members.)

Inquire whether your child's teachers would consider assigning at least two free-choice books to be read during the summer in addition to required reading. (The private schools in our area do this, but my kids' public schools typically require one classic.) An unscientific poll conducted during a moms' coffee at Breughers Bagels revealed that most parents would welcome more assigned summer reading, as long as the kids get to choose the books.

At some schools, principals actively promote a reading culture. They visit classrooms; talk about their favorite books; and read aloud a short, engaging chapter to the class. The kids love it, and it sends the message that reading is important.

Another way you can help promote reading in your child's school is by participating in a parent-teacher organization.

How to Promote Reading through Parent-Teacher Organizations

Parent-teacher organizations (PTOs) welcome volunteers and can encourage reading in a variety of ways. Book promotion is done through a PTO subcommittee, like the Library Committee or the Book Fair Committee, whose members work with the school librarian.

PTOs and school librarians can promote reading by sponsoring a popular YA author visit to the school. Check online to see if authors are speaking at local bookstores, book festivals, or comic-cons.

Authors may be willing to visit your middle or high school if they are in the area. Once you have them scheduled, teachers can assign the author's books or read them out loud during class.

Your PTO could create a "Guess Whose Favorite Book?" board. Ask teachers and principals to submit their favorite young adult books written in the last five years. Take a picture of the book covers and hang them on a wall in front of the cafeteria or some other place students frequent. Write "Guess who?" above all the book covers. After several weeks, reveal which teacher chose which book by placing a photo of the teacher under his or her favorite book.

Book trailers on Booklist or YouTube can be great commercials for new books and get kids talking about what they want to read. They could be shown at the end of lunch before a book fair or before kids leave on summer break. Send links to the book trailers in the PTO or school newsletters. At some schools, kids create book trailers during media class, and the best of them are shown during lunch.

PTOs can promote reading by raffling tickets to an upcoming movie of a popular book like *Ready Player One*. Before *Wonder* came out as a movie, our middle-school-PTO library committee discussed raffling tickets to the movie (including popcorn). In order to enter the raffle, the kids would have to read *Wonder* or *Augie and Me: Three Wonder Stories* and write about their favorite part of the book. The school would show the movie trailer, and the language-arts teachers would do short book chats about the books to get the kids excited about reading.

Book fairs, run by the PTO in conjunction with the school librarian, raise money for the school and promote reading. Middle-school students usually visit the book fair during their language-arts classes. Teachers set up class wish lists so parents can donate books to the classroom library. Many book fairs are now also online, and links can be sent to relatives who may want to buy a book for your child.

To enhance the excitement of a book fair, see if a YA author could attend and sign books. One of our local middle schools hosted Nathan Hale, author of the popular book *One Dead Spy*, during a winter book fair. The kids loved it. School clubs like Destination Imagination can do a donut-sale fundraiser outside of the book fair. (Donuts have a strong track record of increasing book fair attendance.)

A simplified version of a book fair is a one-night fair at Barnes & Noble (B&N), which gives schools 20 percent of the profits in the form of a gift card. In order to maximize attendance, schools hold contests—like the homeroom with the most attendees wins a bagel breakfast. The more student involvement, the better. School bands can perform at the B&N book fair, and school theater groups can act out a scene from an upcoming play. Schools also host art shows and poetry readings during their one-night B&N book fair.

If you are PTO member in a low-income school, partner on literacy projects with teachers who can make funding requests on DonorsChoose.org. In addition, consider applying for grants. See the website PTO Today (www.ptotoday.com), which has articles on finding and winning grants.

Epilogue

Now is the moment to begin a reading project with your children. The benefits of reading are too great to wait. Start by evaluating why your preteen or teen isn't currently reading for pleasure. What's really holding him or her back? Is it a lack of time? Difficulty in finding a good book? A Netflix fixation? Or something else?

Once you identify why your adolescent doesn't read for fun, make adjustments. Help him or her obtain reading material that matches his or her current interests, and carve out time to read. Prompt your adolescent to ask friends and family members for recommendations. Refer to the list of books that hook. Model reading. If necessary, consider using rewards. And establish reading as the most interesting activity in the room. Finally, talk to your adolescent about what he or she reads. Conversation connects us, and reading is even more enjoyable when it's shared.

Resources

Books and Websites of Reading Experts

The books below are written by experienced teachers and reading specialists who are gifted at getting middle-school and high-school students to read for pleasure.

- *The Book Whisperer* and *Reading in the Wild*, by Donalyn Miller. See also Miller's website, www.bookwhisperer.com.
- *Book Love*, by Penny Kittle. See also Kittle's website, www.pennykittle.net.
- *Reading Deeper* and *Readicide*, by Kelly Gallagher. See also Gallagher's website, www.kellygallagher.org.
- *The Read-Aloud Handbook*, by Jim Trelease. See also Trelease's website, www.trelease-on-reading.com.

Websites That Offer Book Recommendations and/or Advice on Encouraging Dormant Readers

- YALSA (www.ala.org/yalsa/booklistsawards/booklistsbook). The Young Adult Library Services Association is a national association of librarians who focus on promoting and strengthening reading for ages twelve to eighteen. On the YALSA website, you can find multiple book lists, including their annual "Best of the Best" books for teens.
- Commonsense.org (https://www.commonsense.org). Offers information on the age appropriateness of books and reading recommendations.
- Scholastic.com (http://www.scholastic.com). Offers articles on books and reading, school success, and recommendations.

Websites for Kids with Learning Differences

- Reading Rockets (http://www.readingrockets.org). Offers information about how parents can help struggling readers.
- Understood (https://www.understood.org). This nonprofit's goal is to help parents who have children with learning and attention issues. Understood has articles on supporting your child's reading at home, partnering with your kid's school, and IEP plans, among many other topics.
- DyslexiaHelp (http://dyslexiahelp.umich.edu). This website is provided by the University of Michigan and contains tips and ideas, activities, success stories, and up-to-date information about dyslexia.

Reading Glossary

<u>Accelerated Reader (AR)</u>: Software for K–12 schools that assesses a student's reading level through the STAR (Standardized Test for the Assessment of Reading) test. Kids get a numerical rating and then pick out books that match their reading level. After they finish a book, they take a quiz on the computer.

<u>annotate</u>: To write down notes about what you are reading. (Teachers often skim students' books looking for their handwritten notes.)

<u>chat fiction</u>: Horror stories read on a smartphone as if the reader was snooping on two characters' texted conversations. Hooked and Yarn are the names of two apps that offer chat fiction.

Crash Course: The author John Green's YouTube video series, which explains English literature, history, and many other subjects.

<u>DEAR (Drop Everything and Read)</u>: A nationwide program that schools implement by having a free reading period during the school day. Students select the books they want to read. See dropeverythingandread.com for more details.

<u>devoted reader:</u> A reader who loves books and typically reads above his or her grade level.

<u>dialect:</u> A dialect is a form of the language that is spoken in a particular part of the country or by a particular group of people.

<u>dormant reader</u>: A kid who is a competent reader but chooses not to read for fun during his or her free time.

<u>dyslexia</u>: A learning disorder that affects a person's ability to read, spell, write, and speak. Kids who have dyslexia are often smart and hardworking.

<u>dystopian fiction</u>: Novels set in a world in which society has completely broken down. (*The Hunger Games* and *Divergent* are examples of dystopian fiction.)

<u>ELA (English language arts), also known as English class</u>: The class where reading, writing, and grammar are taught.

<u>emerging reader</u>: This person is typically reading below his or her grade level. His or her reading struggles may be due to a learning disability, a lack of practice, a lack of mentoring, a lack of confidence, or just a strong dislike for the act of reading.

<u>fanfiction, fanfic</u>: Fanfiction is fiction written by fans of books, TV shows, and movies who make up their own stories about their favorite characters.

<u>fluency</u>: The ability to read quickly and accurately with expression. Teachers often evaluate their students on reading fluency and comprehension.

<u>genres</u>: Groups into which books can be classified. Books in a genre share similar characteristics. Fantasy, realistic fiction, science fiction, and biography are all genres.

<u>graphic novels</u>: These look like comic books but are the length of novels, and teachers, librarians, and Scholastic.com consider them to be real reading.

hi-lo books: High-interest books that have a low page count and lower-level vocabulary words. They are useful for emerging readers who are reading below their grade level.

Lexile: A unit of measurement teachers use to determine the reading level of their students. (See lexile.com for more details.)

manga: Japanese graphic novels.

memoir versus autobiography: An autobiography is written by the author and covers his or her entire life. A memoir, in contrast, covers one aspect of the author's life. (Sometimes these words are used interchangeably, but they are distinct genres.)

middle-grade books: Books written for children in grades six to eight.

reading comprehension: How well you understand what you are reading.

reading flow: When you are so caught up in a book that you don't notice what is going on around you.

Shmoop: Similar to SparkNotes and the Cliff Notes that generation X and older used. This site is frequently accessed by teens for book summaries and analysis.

SparkNotes: A website that provides online book summaries and study guides. According to surveys, the majority of high-school students use SparkNotes or Shmoop, which also offers online summaries.

sustained silent reading (SSR): A school reading program where students self-select books and read them for a set amount of time.

"Three B's": Reading expert Jim Trelease's dictum that there should be books in the bedrooms, books in the bathrooms, and books at the breakfast table.

young adult books: Books for kids between the ages of twelve and eighteen.

Notes

INTRODUCTION

1. Donalyn Miller, *The Book Whisperer* (San Francisco: Jossey-Bass, 2009), 28.

CHAPTER 1: WHY YOU SHOULD ENCOURAGE YOUR KIDS TO READ FOR PLEASURE

1. Frank Bruni, "Read, Kids, Read," *New York Times*, May 12, 2014.

2. Lorene Duzbow, "Watch This. No Read It," *O: The Oprah Magazine*, June 2008, 139-140.

3. Anne E. Cunningham, "What Reading Can Do for the Mind," *Journal of Direct Instruction* 1, no. 2 (Summer 2001): 137–49.

4. Miller, *Book Whisperer*, 55.

5. Michael Breus, "Your Teen Needs More Sleep," *Psychology Today*, September 21, 2017, accessed October 23, 2017, https://www.psychologytoday.com/blog/sleep-newzzz/201709/your-teen-needs-more-sleep.

6. Ibid.

7. The Conference Board, *Are They Really Ready to Work?: Employers' Perspectives on the Basic Knowledge and Applied Skills of New Entrants to the 21st Century U.S. Workforce* (2006), accessed November 28, 2017, http://www.21stcenturyskills.org/documents/FINAL_REPORT_PDF09-29-06.pdf.

8. National Endowment for the Arts, *To Read or Not to Read: A Question of National Consequence*, Reading Report no. 47 (2007), 14–16, accessed November 28, 2017, https://www.arts.gov/sites/default/files/ToRead.pdf.

9. Bowker Market Research, *Understanding the Children's Book Consumer in the Digital Age.*

CHAPTER 2: UNDERSTANDING THE TYPES OF READERS AND PROMOTING READING
1. Jack Jennings, "Can Boys Succeed in Later Life if They Can't Read as Well as Girls?," *Huffington Post*, March 18, 2011, accessed November 28, 2017, https://www.huffingtonpost.com/jack-jennings/can-boys-succeed-in-later_b_837304.html.

CHAPTER 3: READING WITH LEARNING DIFFERENCES
1. Andrew Merle, "The Reading Habits of Ultra-Successful People," *Huffington Post*, April 14, 2016, accessed October 23, 2017, https://www.huffingtonpost.com/andrew-merle/the-reading-habits-of-ult_b_9688130.html.

2. Natasha Postolovski, "The Transformative Effects of Reading + Elon Musk's Reading List," January 21, 2015, accessed October 23, 2017, http://inside.envato.com/the-transformative-effects-of-reading-elon-musks-reading-list/.

CHAPTER 4: WHAT COUNTS AS "REAL" READING?
1. Rich Motoko, "Literacy Debate: Online R U Really Reading?" *New York Times*, July 27, 2008.

2. Karsten Strauss, "These Are the Skills That Bosses Say New College Grads Do Not Have," *Forbes*, May 17, 2016, accessed October 26, 2017,

https://www.forbes.com/sites/karstenstrauss/2016/05/17/these-are-the-skills-bosses-say-new-college-grads-do-not-have/.

3. Ann Patchett, "The Triumph of Readers," *Wall Street Journal*, January 17, 2009.

4. Kelly Gallagher, "Why I Have Brought SparkNotes into My Classroom. And Why You Should Too," *Kelly's Blog* November 30, 2014, accessed November 4, 2017, http://www.kellygal-lagher.org/kellys-blog/2014/11/30/why-i-have-brought-cliffnotes-into-my-classroom-and-why-you-should-too.

5. Kent C. Berridge and Terry E. Robinson, "What Is the Role of Dopamine in Reward: Hedonic Impact, Reward Learning, or Incentive Salience?" *Brain Research Reviews* 28 (1998): 309–18.

6. Daniel H. Pink, *To Sell Is Human* (New York: Riverhead Books, 2012), 100.

Chapter 5: Introducing Reading for Pleasure and Selling Its Benefits
1. Pink, *To Sell Is Human*, 132–33.

2. Ibid., 136.

Chapter 7: Access to Books and Making Reading the Most Interesting Activity in the Room
1. Jim Trelease, "Jim Trelease's Retirement Letter," accessed October 23, 2017, http://www.trelease-on-reading.com/trelease-retirement-letter.html.

CHAPTER 8: READING REWARDS: SHOULD WE USE THEM? DO THEY WORK?
1. Penny Kittle, *Book Love: Developing Strength, Stamina, and Passion in Adolescent Readers* (Portsmouth, NH: Heinennann, 2013).

CHAPTER 9: SUMMER READING AND TRAVELING WITH BOOKS, AUDIOBOOKS, AND PODCASTS
1. Jimmy Kim, interview in "Summer by the Book," *Usable Knowledge*, June 25, 2015, accessed October 24, 2017, https://www.gse.harvard.edu/news/uk/15/06/summer-book.

2. Bill Gates, "My Favorite Books of 2016," *Gates Notes* (blog), December 5, 2016, accessed October 24, 2017, https://www.gatesnotes.com/About-Bill-Gates/Best-Books-2016.

3. W. Greg McCall and C. Craig, "Same-Language-Subtitling (SLS): Using Subtitled Music Video for Reading Growth," Association for the Advancement of Computers in Education (EDMEDIA), January 11, 2009, accessed November 29, 2017, http://www.same-language-subtitling.com/paper-sls.html.

CHAPTER 10: READING FOR PLEASURE WHEN SCHOOL RESUMES
1. Common Core States Standard Initiative, "Language Arts State Standards, Reading Informational Texts, Grade 8," Commoncore.org, accessed October 28, 2017, http://www.corestandards.org/ELA-Literacy/RI/8/.

2. H. Anderson, "How Shakespeare Influences the Way We Speak Now," BBC.com, October 21, 2014, accessed on November 2, 2017, http://www.bbc.com/culture/story/20140527-say-what-shakespeares-words.

Chapter 11: Book Clubs Encourage Reading—but Will Your Adolescent Join One?

1. Jean M. Twenge, "Have Smartphones Destroyed a Generation?" *The Atlantic*, September 2017, accessed December 10, 2017, https://www.theatlantic.com/magazine/archive/2017/09/has-the-smartphone-destroyed-a-generation/534198.

2. Judith Newman, "Dear Book Club: It's You, Not Me," *New York Times*, May 11, 2017.

Chapter 12: Reading Real and Fake News: Why You Should Care Whether Your Kid Can Tell the Difference

1. International Federation of Library Associations, "How to Spot Fake News," August 13, 2017, accessed November 28, 2017, https://www.ifla.org/publications/node/11174.

About the Author

Kaye Newton lives outside Nashville with her husband, her three children, and two lively dogs. Her first book, *Incision Decisions*, won a silver medal at the 2017 Readers' Favorites Awards. Keep up with Kaye at Kayenewton.com.

A Note from the Author

Thank you for reading my book! I hope you found *How to Get Your Screen-Loving Kids to Read Books for Pleasure* informative. If you did, please consider leaving a review online so that others can discover it. Together, we can build a community of readers.

70347640R00102

Made in the USA
Middletown, DE
13 April 2018